KŌ 候

JAPANESE MICROSEASONS

KŌ 候

JAPANESE MICROSEASONS

FIND CALM IN THE 72 MICROSEASONS OF THE JAPANESE CALENDAR

ANTONIO ANTEFERMO

RIZZOLI UNIVERSE

Published in 2026 by
Rizzoli Universe, a division of
Rizzoli International Publications

Rizzoli International Publications Inc
49 West 27th Street
New York, NY 10001

Rizzoli International Publications UK Ltd
Somerset House, West Wing
Strand, London WC2R 1LA

www.rizzoliusa.com

Original title: *Il linguaggio segreto delle stagioni. Vivere al ritmo del Giappone* © 2024 Giunti Editore S.p.A., Firenze-Milano. www.giunti.it

publisher: Charles Miers
associate publisher: Tina Persaud
senior editor: Kristy Richardson
design: Wayne Blades
reproduction: Rival UK
production manager: Michelle Wells

A CIP catalogue record for this book is available from the British Library.

ISBN: 9780789346780
2026 / 1

Printed in China

MIX
Paper | Supporting responsible forestry
FSC™ C005748

The authorized representative in the EU for safety and compliance is Mondadori Libri S.p.A.,via Gian Battista Vico 42, Milan, Italy, 20123, www.mondadori.it

Visit us online: Instagram.com/RizzoliBooks
Facebook.com/RizzoliNewYork
Youtube.com/user/RizzoliNY

To my wife, for her unconditional love, endless patience, and tireless support. Thank you for being my compass and constant inspiration in every step of this journey.

To my son, for his curiosity and zest for life which remind me every day of the importance of seeing the world with new eyes full of wonder.

CONTENTS

SPRING

SUMMER

AUTUMN

WINTER

RITTŌ: WINTER HAS BEGUN

SHŌSETSU: FIRST SNOW WHITENS THE GROUND

TAISETSU: THICK SNOW FALLS

TŌJI: THE WINTER SOLSTICE

SHŌKAN: COLD ENVELOPS THE WORLD

DAIKAN: THE COLDEST TIME

INTRODUCTION

The idea for this book came from my passion for the East and my training as a psychologist and practitioner of martial arts and meditation. For years I have been immersing myself in Japanese culture, fascinated by its ability to harmoniously combine tradition and modernity, rigor and beauty, discipline and contemplation. Almost by chance, during my research, I discovered the traditional Japanese calendar, which divides the year into periods of about five days, each characterized by a particular natural phenomenon. This way of observing the changing seasons struck me deeply, offering a new way of seeing the world and living in tune with the rhythms of nature. As a psychologist, I have always sought tools that can help people live fuller and more fulfilling lives. By integrating the principles of Buddhism, mindfulness, and Acceptance and Commitment Therapy (ACT) with the observation of microseasons, I have found an effective method to promote mental well-being and personal growth. Being mindful of small seasonal changes invites us to reflect on our lives, accept the transience of experiences, and cultivate resilience.

The practice of martial arts has taught me the importance of discipline, concentration, and inner strength. These teachings, combined with meditation, have helped me to develop a balanced approach to life, which I now wish to share with you through this book.

MY ZEN PSYCHOLOGY

My Zen psychology approach integrates the principles of Buddhism with modern psychological methods for mental well-being, such as ACT, mindfulness, and self-compassion. This method of intervention helps people learn more about themselves and the world, effectively dealing with the challenges of daily life.

ACT, a type of therapy based on acceptance and committed action, is a scientifically based model that aims to increase psychological flexibility, to improve personal well-being, and help people live a rich and fulfilling life. Building a flexible mind means developing the ability to adapt and respond effectively to different situations in life.

Mindfulness is a practice that invites us to be fully present in the here and now, observing our thoughts and emotions without judgment. It helps us to develop a greater connection with ourselves and the world around us, fostering calmness and mental clarity.

Self-compassion involves treating ourselves with the same kindness and understanding that we would offer to a close friend. This practice helps us cultivate a loving attitude toward ourselves, reducing judgment and self-criticism.

Each of the 72 microseasons of the Japanese calendar offers us a unique opportunity for reflection and learning and permits us to explore how these principles can be applied in daily life.

THE TRADITIONAL JAPANESE CALENDAR

The traditional Japanese calendar is an ancient system that divides the year into 24 solar terms, called *Nijūshi Sekki* (二十四節気), each lasting about 15 days. This calendar, originally adopted by China, has been refined in Japan to reflect seasonal changes in more detail than the four main seasons. To make this observation even more precise, each solar term was divided into three microseasons, thus creating a total of 72 microseasons, or *Shichijūni Kō* (七十二候). Each microseason lasts about five days and captures natural changes in detail. These microseasons include events such as the budding of flowers, the arrival of swallows, or the first frost. Each represents a more intimate way to connect with the natural world, but also a unique time of the year, marked by specific phenomena and environmental changes.

The traditional Japanese calendar is not only a tool for measuring time, but is deeply rooted in Japanese culture and spirituality. Each microseason brings with it observations and reflections that have inspired poets, artists, and philosophers throughout the centuries. The *Kō* represents an invitation to live in harmony with natural rhythms, to observe carefully the changes in our environment, and to reflect on how they affect our inner life. Learning to live in rhythm with this calendar can enrich our daily lives, encouraging us to slow down and appreciate the small changes around us. It invites us to pay attention to details and find beauty and meaning in the small things. This approach can also improve our mental and spiritual well-being.

LIVING TO THE RHYTHM OF THE MICROSEASONS

Each *Kō* lasts about five days and describes a specific natural phenomenon. This level of detail allows us to observe and appreciate the subtle but important changes that take place in nature, reminding us of its constant evolution, as well as the significance and purpose of each of these periods.

The traditional Japanese calendar also reflects the life cycle of birth, growth, decline, and renewal. Each microseason represents a specific time in this cycle, offering a metaphor for our personal and spiritual growth. Following the rhythm of the microseasons invites us to develop a greater awareness of the natural world and our place within it. It encourages us to slow down and observe seasonal changes, to reflect on how they affect our lives, and to live in harmony with natural rhythms. This approach can help us find balance and serenity, accepting change as a natural and necessary part of life.

The *Kō* offers us valuable life lessons, teaching us qualities such as patience, resilience, and the ability to adapt to change. In essence, the system of 72 microseasons not only celebrates the beauty and complexity of the natural cycle, but also offers us a model for living more consciously and harmoniously.

HAIKU

In this book, each *Sekki* opens with a haiku I have written myself, inspired by the solar term described. Haiku is a form of traditional

Japanese poetry that captures ephemeral moments of nature and daily life in three lines. These short verses, traditionally composed of 17 mora (short syllables), arranged in three lines of 5, 7, and 5 mora, are celebrated for their depth and simplicity. The strict and concise structure of haiku requires careful word choice intended to evoke vivid images and intense feelings. This limited structure is enough to paint a rich and meaningful picture of nature or everyday life. Haiku often include a *kigo*, a seasonal word that connects the poem to a particular time of year, and a *kireji*, a word that creates a pause or caesura, adding depth and reflection to the text. In the contemporary world, many poets choose not to rigidly follow the 5-7-5 pattern. This flexibility allows for greater creativity while maintaining the brevity of haiku. Variation in structure can allow a freer interpretation of the moments captured and an accurate representation of the emotions and images one wishes to evoke.

Composing haiku is not only a writing exercise, but also a meditative practice that can have numerous psychological benefits.

- Writing haiku requires concentration and being fully present in the moment. Observing nature and describing its subtle nuances helps us to develop awareness and live in the present with greater intensity.
- The act of creating haiku can be relaxing and therapeutic. Taking time to reflect on the beauty of nature and translating these observations into words can relieve stress.
- Haiku offers a simple but powerful way to express deep emotions and feelings. Writing about moments of beauty, change, and transience can help us process personal experiences and find a sense of peace.
- Composing haiku strengthens the connection with nature. This connection leads to a greater appreciation for the environment and a sense of belonging to the cycle of life.

HOW TO USE THIS BOOK

This book is designed as a practical guide to help you integrate the principles of Zen psychology into your daily life, inspired by Japan's cycle of 72 microseasons. Here are some suggestions on how to get the most out of your reading.

- **Explore the microseasons**: Although the Western and Japanese seasons may not coincide exactly, the universal principles of nature and change are applicable everywhere. Adapt the reflections to your local reality, finding parallels and connections with your personal context. My advice is to read this book in rhythm with the microseasons, using the Japanese calendar to create a program for growth.
- **Practical exercises**: At the end of each section, you will find exercises to put the concepts discussed into practice. These helpful exercises will guide you through mindfulness practices, personal reflection, and activities for growth.
- **Haiku and reflection**: Each *Sekki* is introduced by a haiku, a short poem that captures the essence of that period. Read the haiku carefully and be inspired by the images and feelings that it evokes. You can also try to write your own haiku as a form of personal expression and meditation.
- **Integrate into everyday life**: The teachings in this book are not meant to remain only on paper. Try to integrate the principles of each microseason into your daily life. Whether this is developing patience, cultivating resilience, or finding beauty in small moments, apply these concepts in the way that best fits your life.
- **Keep a journal**: Keeping a journal of your reflections, haiku, and experiences with the exercises can be a way to monitor your progress and deepen your practice. Re-reading your entries over time will allow you to see how you have grown and changed.

- **Mindfulness practice**: Use this book as a tool to develop an ongoing mindfulness practice. Take time each day to stop and reflect on the lessons of the current microseason. This daily practice will help you stay connected to the natural rhythm of life.

Remember that this book is a traveling companion on your journey of growth. Approach it with an open heart and an inquisitive mind and let the teachings inspired by the Japanese microseasons guide you toward a more conscious and meaningful life.

Happy reading
Antonio, the Zen psychologist

NOTE

The translation of the names of the microseasons in this book is the result of careful personal research. However, it is important to remember that some *kanji* (the ideograms used in Japanese writing to express a concept or word) lend themselves to different interpretations, and for this reason you may encounter slightly different translations elsewhere.

In addition, the dates given for each microseason are based on an adaptation to the Gregorian calendar. These dates should be considered approximate, as they may differ slightly from those of the traditional Japanese calendar. This discrepancy is due to the differences between the Japanese lunisolar calendar and the Gregorian solar calendar, as well as differences in latitude and climatic conditions.

SPRING BEGINS

立春

Risshun

SHY SHOOTS,
WHISPERS
THE MARCH WIND,
PROMISE OF FLOWERS.

FEBRUARY 4–8

EAST WINDS MELT THE ICE

東風解凍 *Harukaze kōri o toku*

As the winds of the East melt the ice, so kindness dissolves the barriers of the heart. Let the warmth of compassion touch everything you encounter.

The arrival of spring, marked by the rush of warm winds that melt ice, offers a time for deep reflection on the dynamics of transformation and renewal. This seasonal change not only alters the external landscape but can also serve as a powerful metaphor for the inner changes that many of us desire or need.

Melting ice is not simply a physical phenomenon; it also represents the letting go of mental and emotional rigidities. In our lives, we may accumulate emotional blocks or resistance that prevent us from moving forward and expressing ourselves freely—these can be compared to ice forming in the depths of winter. The melting process can then be seen as symbolizing the release of such obstacles, allowing us to flow more freely toward our more authentic goals and desires. Kindness and compassion are essential tools in this process of inner transformation. Just as the warm winds of the East facilitate the natural transition from harsh winter temperatures to spring rebirth, so an attitude of kindness toward oneself and others can help to mitigate and finally dissolve emotional barriers. Compassion, in particular, allows us to face and accept vulnerabilities of our own and of other people, fostering an inner and a social environment where change can occur more smoothly and naturally.

This period of transformation emphasizes the importance of being open to ongoing change. By accepting that change is a natural part of existence, as shown by seasonal cycles, we can adapt more easily to new life circumstances. In addition, recognizing that every ending is a new beginning helps us remain resilient and optimistic in the face of challenges, viewing every obstacle as an opportunity to grow and evolve.

INCORPORATING KINDNESS AND COMPASSION INTO DAILY LIFE Showing kindness to yourself and others is a way of strengthening personal bonds and making every day a source of positive good.

- **Self-compassion:** Start with yourself. Practice self-compassion by forgiving yourself for past mistakes and accepting your imperfections. Remember that every person has his or her flaws, and that the path to self-acceptance is a life-enriching journey.
- **Active listening:** Show kindness and compassion by actively listening to others and offering your presence without judgment. This kind of listening creates a safe space for expression and sharing, strengthening bonds and promoting deeper understanding and connection.
- **Compassionate action:** Engage in compassionate actions throughout your day. This can range from simple acts of everyday kindness (such as helping a neighbor) to volunteering for good causes. Each action counts and has the effect of further spreading kindness and compassion in the world.

FEBRUARY 9–13

NIGHTINGALES SING THEIR SONG OVER THE MOUNTAINS

黄鶯睍睆 *Kōō kenkan su*

Birdsong in the morning awakens our hearts and fills them with hope and joy. Be bold in singing your own melody.

This microseason is symbolic of nature's awakening, inspiring us to reflect on the power of our inner voice. Nightingale song serves as a metaphor for authenticity in self-expression, which is essential for a full and fulfilled life. It is a spontaneous phenomenon; it is not influenced by external concerns or desires for appreciation. Similarly, our most authentic expression emerges when we free ourselves from the expectations of others, freely manifesting thoughts, feelings, and creativity. Birdsong is known for its ability to elevate the mood and bring joy to the listener. Similarly, when we use our voice authentically, we have the power to influence others positively, offering inspiration and consolation.

Being authentic requires courage, especially when this implies sharing ideas that might be poorly received. However, learning to communicate without fear is a foundational step toward personal fulfillment. This act of courage not only strengthens our self-esteem but also lights the way for others.

MEDITATION ON SOUNDS Find a moment in your day to sit outside, perhaps in a garden, a park, or even just next to an open window.

1. Close your eyes and focus on the sounds around you. Listen to the sounds of nature. If you are lucky, you will be able to hear birds singing. If that is not possible, pay attention to other natural sounds.
2. As you listen, reflect on the qualities of sound. Think about how birdsong or the sounds of nature can sound spontaneous and authentic.
3. After listening for a few minutes, take a moment to express yourself creatively. You can write a short poem, paint or draw, sing, or play an instrument.
4. As you express yourself, focus on your emotions and notice how you feel without judging or repressing them.
5. Finally, reflect on your experience. Take a moment to reflect on what you have just done. Use a notebook or tablet to record your thoughts. Think about how you can integrate this practice into your daily life.

FEBRUARY 14–18

FISH PEEP OUT OF THE ICE

魚上氷 *Uo kōri o izuru*

Even beneath the coldest and stillest surface, life is poised to emerge and continue its journey. Never underestimate the strength that is contained within you.

This microseason tells us about resilience and the ability to push through challenges. The fish emerging from the ice reminds us that no matter how tough a situation may seem, there is always movement and possibility beneath the surface. It is a reminder of the possibility of cultivating hope and resilience, even when we feel stuck. It is a quality we all possess; like fish under the ice, we are never completely still or trapped. There is always potential for movement, growth, and transformation.

The surfacing fish symbolize tenacity and the ability to find a way through even the most difficult situations. This time of year invites us to look beyond the barrier of our personal difficulties, encouraging us to find the inner strength to break through the ice that holds us back and continue swimming toward new horizons.

In Japanese culture, nature is often seen as a guide for human life. We therefore welcome this microseason as an opportunity to reflect on our ability to adapt and consider our inner strength.

Let's use this period to meditate on how to emerge from our challenges with renewed hope and determination, knowing that, just like the fish, we have within ourselves the ability to overcome any obstacle.

BREAKING THE ICE This exercise aims to transform your perception of your challenges by encouraging you to recognize and overcome emotional or situational blocks through concrete actions with renewed hope. Find a quiet time and space to reflect without interruptions. Make sure to have a pen and paper with you.

1. Think of an aspect of your life where you feel stuck. It may be related to work, relationships, or a goal that you think is unattainable. On a sheet of paper, express these feelings or scenarios. Write without judging. Now, take this paper and put it under something heavy (a large book, a vase, or something else). Let it stay there for a few hours or even overnight. This act will help you create a physical metaphor for the "emotional load" that is holding you back.
2. When you feel ready, return to your paper. Carefully remove the heavy object. This gesture symbolizes recognition and acceptance of your challenges.
3. Now, tear the paper into pieces. As you do so, imagine getting rid of the limitations you have identified. Think of it as a symbol of you emerging through challenges, just like the fish finding the strength to climb up through the ice into the light.
4. Spend a few moments reflecting on the liberating feeling of this gesture. Ask yourself how you can apply this resilience and determination to overcoming obstacles in your real life. Think about the steps you plan to take, inspired by the tenacity of the fish under the ice.

SNOW MELTS AND RAIN FALLS

雨水

Usui

SILENT THE RAIN,
IT TOUCHES THE FIRST
WHITE FLOWERS,
WAKES THE EARTH.

FEBRUARY 19–23

THE RAIN MOISTENS THE SOIL

土脉潤起 *Tsuchi no shō uruoi okoru*

Every raindrop that bathes the earth reminds us that even after the driest times, rebirth and new opportunities always follow.

Just as rain nourishes the soil, making it fertile for future growth, in the same way our experiences, whether bright or shrouded in shadow, shape and enrich our being in profound and meaningful ways. Every event, every encounter, every challenge we face carries with it the potential for personal growth and inner transformation.

Imagine a day of heavy rain, when the sky seems to pour its full force upon us. At first it may seem frustrating, annoying, even overwhelming. But after the rain, the air is cleaner, the colors of nature are more vivid, and the earth is ready to welcome new seeds. Similarly, even the most difficult and painful experiences may seem unbearable at first, but with time, they purify our minds and spirits, revealing new opportunities for growth and beauty.

Embracing each moment of life means gratefully and openly accepting the lessons it offers us, knowing that even the most difficult circumstances conceal seeds of new beginnings and unexpected possibilities. It is in the fabric of our experiences that we discover our resilience, strength, and adaptability, qualities that allow us to flourish even in the most challenging conditions.

Remember that continuous transformation is the very essence of human existence; we are created to evolve, change, and grow, just like the nature around us. Embracing this process means dancing to the rhythm of change, keeping your heart open to the endless possibilities that each new day brings. Thus, step by step, we learn to see each experience as a precious gift, a piece that contributes to building the mosaic of our lives, rich in color, nuance, and depth.

On this journey, let the rain of your experiences irrigate the soil of your spirit, preparing it to welcome new flowers. Try to see every day, every moment, as an opportunity to grow, learn, and transform. Celebrate this process, knowing that every step you take contributes to your wonderful evolution.

THE RAIN JAR Take a moment to reflect on recent experiences that have nourished your spirit. Create a virtual rain jar by writing these experiences on small pieces of paper. Whenever you feel in need of comfort or inspiration, take a piece of paper from the jar to remind yourself how each experience contributes to your growth.

FEBRUARY 24–28

THE FOG BEGINS TO DESCEND

霞始靆 *Kasumi hajimete tanabiku*

Even when fog obscures the path ahead, remember that each step brings you closer to your final destination. Trust the journey, even when you can't see where you are heading.

Foggy days teach us to keep calm and continue moving forward, trusting the process and listening to our intuition. The fog, with its mysterious veil that shrouds everything, prevents us from seeing the road ahead clearly. However, if we change our perspective, we recognize a silent teacher in the fog. It teaches us to slow down, to pay attention to our steps, and to trust the path we are on, even if the final destination remains hidden from sight. Developing this kind of trust requires courage, patience, and a deep faith in ourselves and the process of life. Embracing uncertainty makes us more aware. Instead of struggling to see beyond it, we learn to appreciate the landscape around us, discovering beauty and details we would otherwise have overlooked. This process opens us up to new and unexpected experiences.

Moreover, the fog reminds us that, although we may have plans and goals, life itself is inherently unpredictable. This realization frees us from the pressure to control every aspect of our existence. Instead, it invites us to trust our ability to navigate the unknown, the people who walk alongside us, and every step we take.

Thus, as we advance through the fog of life, we treasure its lessons. The fog, then, is not only a teacher, but also a symbol of our ability to face the unknown with hope and optimism, reminding us that each step forward is an act of faith in the extraordinary journey of life.

WALKING THROUGH THE FOG This exercise will help you find calm when you feel overwhelmed by uncertainty for the future. Walking through fog is a metaphor that will teach you to walk confidently, focusing only on the next step.

1. Choose a safe and quiet space, outdoors or indoors, where you can walk undisturbed. Stand still and close your eyes for a few moments. Take some deep breaths. Visualize a light mist enveloping the space around you.
2. Open your eyes and start walking very slowly forward. Focus on each step you take: how your foot touches the ground; the movement of your legs; the change of weight from one foot to the other. Imagine that with each step, the fog around you becomes slightly clearer, symbolizing your ability to move through uncertainty with greater confidence.
3. After a while, slow down to a stop. Close your eyes and take a few deep breaths, reconnecting with your internal state. Reflect on how you feel now compared to before the exercise.
4. End your walk in the fog with a moment of gratitude for taking this time to heal yourself. When you feel ready, open your eyes and slowly return to your daily activities, taking this sense of calm with you.

MARCH 1–5

GRASS SPROUTS, TREES BUD

草木萌動 *Sōmoku mebae izuru*

Every shoot that emerges from the ground is a sign of perseverance and rebirth. Be like the shoot that, even in the face of challenges, finds the strength to grow toward the light.

Nature, with its timeless resilience and ability to adapt and thrive even in the most adverse and inhospitable of conditions, offers us an inexhaustible source of inspiration and wisdom.

Observing a flower growing through a crack in concrete or a tree growing in rocky ground reminds us that every being, at its deepest core, is driven by a life force that always seeks the light, despite obstacles. This same life force also flows through us, endowing us with an intrinsic resilience that enables us to overcome challenges, adapt to changing circumstances, and ultimately flourish. Recognizing and trusting this natural resilience is essential to our personal and spiritual development.

Each of us possesses a unique potential for growth, a seed of possibility that, when nurtured with care, patience, and determination, can blossom into something truly extraordinary. Allowing ourselves to bloom means fully accepting who we are, including our imperfections and vulnerabilities, and embracing the lessons each experience teaches us.

Trusting one's potential for growth also requires the courage to let go of fears, doubts, and limiting expectations that can stifle our ability to develop. It is an invitation to live authentically, following one's values, passions, and curiosities, even when that means straying from the established path or facing uncertainty. When we allow ourselves to be guided by our inner truth and inherent potential, we begin to flourish in ways beyond our imagination. In this flowering process, it is important to remember that we are not alone. Just as nature is interconnected in an intricate web of relationships and mutual support, so we grow through connections with others. Cultivating meaningful relationships, seeking inspiration and support from our community, and offering our help to others are all key activities that nourish our spirit and accelerate our personal growth.

So, as we proceed on our life journey, let us be inspired by the resilience and beauty of nature around us. Let us trust our inherent ability to overcome obstacles, adapt, and thrive. Let us give ourselves permission to explore all our wonderful possibilities, remembering that just as each seed contains the potential to become a magnificent flower, so each individual possesses all that is necessary to flourish fully in their uniqueness and beauty.

THE SEED OF LIFE Plant a seed in a pot and observe it every day. Reflect on the metaphor of the growing sprout: it requires time, patience, and care to grow through the dark soil. Note the changes you observe and how they are reflected in your personal or professional goals.

THE DAY OF INSECT AWAKENING

啓蟄

Keichitsu

UNDER THE MOIST LEAF,
A CHORUS OF SMALL LIFE,
TEEMING AWAKENING.

MARCH 6–10

INSECTS EMERGE FROM THEIR BURROWS

蟄虫啓戸 *Sugomori mushito or hiraku*

Every awakening, after a period of rest and reflection, brings with it the potential for new life and new discoveries. Be open to the transformations that await.

The period of awakening and renewal when insects emerge from their burrows into a new cycle of life is a powerful symbol of transformation that we also find in our human experience. This metaphor borrowed from nature invites us to reflect on the capacity for rebirth that lies dormant in each of us, just waiting to be awakened. Like nature renewing itself, leaving behind winter hibernation to burst into new life with spring, we too are called to reconsider our inner shelters: those safe but often limiting places where we seek refuge out of fear of the new or the unknown. These shelters can take the form of old habits and beliefs, relationships that no longer enrich us, or simply comfort zones that prevent us from exploring our full potential.

The invitation to let go of what no longer serves us is actually an invitation to freedom, to discover new challenges, to explore new horizons. This requires courage, since embracing change means facing the uncertainty that the future holds. However, it is through this process of opening up and abandoning the known for the unknown that true growth occurs.

Each awakening, therefore, becomes an opportunity to reinvent ourselves, experiment, learn, and ultimately grow. It is a cycle of renewal that allows us to live more fully, to express our true essence and potential. In this sense, each ending becomes not a cause for sadness, but an opening to new adventures and exciting experiences. This process is not a one-time occurrence, but rather a continuous cycle that characterizes the entire course of our existence. Learning to navigate it gracefully is essential for a balanced and fulfilling life. By embracing the natural cycle of rest and renewal we align with the rhythms of life itself, finding harmony in the change and beauty in the process of transformation.

Remember, every end is only the beginning of something new and potentially wonderful. It is through this eternal cycle of death and rebirth that we discover who we are and what we can become.

YOUR INNER REFUGE Take a moment to reflect on the internal shelters you may have built to keep yourself safe from fear of the unknown or the new, be they attitudes, beliefs, or relationships that no longer serve you. Write or draw these "safe places" on a piece of paper, then tear it up symbolically as a gesture of liberation and openness to the new.

MARCH 11–15

THE FIRST PEACH BLOSSOMS

桃始笑 *Momo hajimete saku*

Just as the first peach blossoms herald the arrival of spring, so each small step forward marks the initiation of new growth. Celebrate each progression.

The arrival of the first peach blossoms marks a delicate and powerful transition in nature. The blossoming of these trees, with their vibrant colors and sweet fragrance, joyfully announces the imminent spring, but it also brings with it profound metaphors for each individual's path of personal and spiritual growth. It teaches us, in fact, the importance of patience and perseverance. After months of cold winter weather, in which the trees seem dormant and lifeless, the peach blossoms bloom against all odds, transforming the landscape into a vibrant canvas of color. Similarly, there are times in our lives when we might feel stagnant or dormant during the cold "winter" of our personal challenges. At such times we may doubt that "spring" will ever come. However, just like peach blossoms, we too possess the innate ability to overcome periods of darkness and bloom again.

Not only that: the first peach blossoms spur us on to find joy and gratitude in the small advances and moments of beauty that dot our path. In a world that often exclusively values the achievement of big goals and immediate success, peach blossoms whisper the importance of celebrating every small victory and every small step forward. These moments, though they may seem insignificant in the grand scheme of things, are critical to our emotional well-being and continued growth. They teach us to appreciate the journey as much as the destination, recognizing that every step in the process is precious and worthy of our celebration.

In addition, peach blossoms symbolize hope and renewal, reminding us that no matter how hard the winter season of our lives may have been, spring always comes. They encourage us to maintain hope even in difficult times, knowing that renewal is always on the horizon. They urge us to remain open and receptive to change, ready to welcome new opportunities and experiences.

So, as we contemplate the first peach blossoms, let us be inspired by their resilience, beauty, and promise of renewal. Their wisdom reminds us to embrace small advances, celebrate each step of our growth journey, and keep alive the hope in the infinite potential that each new season brings us.

Like peach blossoms, we too can blossom in all our beauty, one step at a time, confident in the magnificent unfolding of our lives.

PROGRESS JOURNAL Create a progress journal where you jot down each day a small success, a new discovery about yourself, or a moment of joy. This will help you focus on the positive aspects of your life and recognize your personal growth over time.

MARCH 16–20

CATERPILLARS TURN INTO BUTTERFLIES

菜虫化蝶 *Namushi chō to naru*

All change, even the most profound, begins with a small step and feeds on time and care. Accept every moment with patience, knowing that each transformation is simply a step toward your true essence.

The metamorphosis from caterpillar to butterfly embodies a profound metaphor for our path of personal evolution. This natural process teaches us that periods of stillness and introspection are not just moments of waiting, but stages that prelude personal successes. Our lives reflect this cycle of death and rebirth, of endings and new beginnings. In the cocoon stage, the caterpillar is not simply waiting; it is also undergoing a radical transformation. Similarly, the periods when we feel isolated or in transition are often when we are undergoing the most profound changes. These times of introspection and withdrawal from the world allow us to reconnect with our deepest selves, reflect on our path, and prepare for our next phase of growth.

Society often values constant action and visible results, but metamorphosis requires patience, time, and a secure space. By allowing ourselves time to evolve, we are creating a fertile environment for our transformation, allowing the most authentic version of ourselves to emerge. Moreover, the transformation from caterpillar to butterfly teaches us that each stage of our life has its own purpose and beauty. The caterpillar, with its seemingly modest existence, is just as vital as the butterfly. Finally, the flight of the butterfly out of its cocoon invites us to spread our wings and share our unique essence with the world, showing us the beauty of personal accomplishments after periods of deep reflection and inner metamorphosis.

TAKING FLIGHT This exercise will help you reflect on the transformations you are experiencing or wish to experience in your life.

1. Find a quiet place where you will not be disturbed. Sit comfortably and close your eyes. Breathe deeply to center yourself and relax.
2. With your eyes closed, begin to visualize yourself as a caterpillar. Imagine that you are safe in your cocoon, in the presence of a transformation. Think about the qualities the caterpillar must have at this stage: patience; trust in the process; the courage to leave behind the old for the new. Think about areas of your life where you desire or are already experiencing transformation. Ask yourself, "What are the essential elements I need to support this transformation of mine?"
3. Open your eyes and start writing down your reflections. Note down the transformations you desire, the resources you need, and any actions you can take to facilitate the process. Also consider the obstacles you will encounter and how to overcome them, keeping a constructive perspective. At the end of your reflection, choose a concrete action that will move you closer to your transformation. It can be something as simple as devoting more time to yourself, or seeking support from friends or professionals.
4. Close the exercise with a moment of gratitude for dedicating this time to your growth. Remember that every step is precious. In the same way the caterpillar becomes a butterfly, you too have the innate ability to transform and flourish in all your magnificent potential.

THE SPRING EQUINOX

春分

Shunbun

EQUAL DAY AND NIGHT,
FLEETING BALANCE,
LARK'S SONG.

MARCH 21–25

SPARROWS BEGIN TO NEST

雀始巣 *Suzume hajimete sukū*

As sparrows carefully weave their nests, so we can build our lives, branch by branch, with love and dedication.

The image of sparrows intent on building their nests reflects a universal need for security, love, and belonging, which are also fundamental for human beings. The metaphor leads us to reflect not only on the physical spaces we inhabit but also on our inner shelters and the materials we choose to build them. Each branch represents a choice, habit, relationship, or belief that we decide to weave into the structure. The quality of these materials determines the strength and comfort of our nest, affecting our ability to weather the storms of life. Choosing strong and flexible branches, such as kindness, resilience, open-mindedness, and compassion, will make our nest a place of shelter and growth. In contrast, materials such as hostility, isolation, fear, or intransigence will make our shelter insecure and unstable.

The nest is not only a physical shelter but also a symbol of the relationships we cultivate. Just as sparrows collaborate in nest building, so we also create shared spaces of mutual support, love, and understanding. This period reminds us to nurture relationships that enrich our nest.

Finally, our nest is the place where we retreat to find peace, silence, and connection with our true self. Nurturing this sanctuary allows us to recharge, reflect, and grow.

THE INNER NEST This exercise is designed to help you create an internal refuge where you can find shelter in difficult times.

1. Find a place where you will not be disturbed. Turn off electronic devices and let people know you need some quiet time. Sit down and close your eyes. Take time to focus on your breath.

2. Imagine that you are in a safe place. This will be the site of your nest. It can be a real place or a figment of your imagination. Observe yourself beginning to build your nest. Notice the details: is it in a tree, in a cozy corner, or under a starry sky?
3. Reflect on qualities to include in your nest: branches representing serenity, joy, resilience, love, or any other value important to you. Visualize these as you gather the branches, one by one, and weave them into your nest. In addition to the qualities, you can add elements such as a cherished object, the colors of the sunset, the sound of flowing water, the smell of rain, or a field of flowers. Create a haven where you can be yourself, free from judgments and fears.
4. Imagine sitting or lying down in your nest. Feel the support and love you have woven into each branch. Enjoy the peace of your nest. Remember that it is a place you can always return to.
5. When you feel ready, bring your attention back to the present. Take a moment to reflect on the exercise. You may want to note down your feelings, thoughts, and inspirations.
6. Take a few minutes each day to visit your nest. You can add new branches or enjoy the peace it offers. The nest is a refuge in our mind, where we can find balance, calm, and strength.

MARCH 26–30

THE CHERRY TREE STARTS TO BLOOM

櫻始開 *Sakura hajimete saku*

Each petal that opens in the sun is a reminder of the ephemeral beauty of life; let us grasp each moment with gratitude and wonder.

In Japan, the blooming of the cherry blossom is a cherished event as a symbol of ephemeral beauty, rebirth, and new life. That brief but intense period of natural splendor brings with it profound lessons about the transience of life and the importance of seizing the moment and beauty in its many forms. The flower, with its delicate, pink and white petals, becomes a metaphor for how life, though sometimes short, is full of precious moments that deserve to be lived with intensity and gratitude.

LIVING IN THE PRESENT MOMENT

The ephemeral nature of cherry blossom teaches us to value the present moment. At a time when we are constantly distracted by commitments, notifications, and expectations, stopping to admire the beauty of the cherry blossom reminds us to slow down. It is an invitation to put aside worries about the future or regrets about the past and to fully experience the uniqueness of each moment.

THE PRECIOUSNESS OF LIFE

Each cherry blossom flower is a reminder of how precious life is. Their blooming, so rapid and fleeting, symbolizes the vulnerability and transience of human existence. This awareness can inspire us to live with greater intensity, appreciating the small daily joys, valuing relationships, and pursuing our dreams with passion and determination.

WELCOMING EVERY EXPERIENCE

Cherry blossom also invites us to welcome every experience with openness. Just as we welcome the beauty of the cherry blossom, so we can learn to gratefully accept every aspect of our lives, including challenges and difficulties. Acceptance does not mean resignation, but rather a deep awareness that every experience, joy, or sorrow contributes to our personal growth.

REFLECTION AND RENEWAL

Finally, the flowering of the cherry blossom marks a period of rebirth and renewal. It is a time to reflect on changes to be made, dreams to be pursued, and habits to be cultivated. This phase of natural splendor is an invitation to reflect on our own existence, to reconnect with ourselves and the world around us, and to live each day with intention, gratitude, and presence.

OBSERVE WITH THE HEART Take a moment each day to observe something beautiful in your environment, be it a flower, the sky, a work of art, or perhaps someone's smile. Breathe deeply and allow yourself to be completely absorbed by what is in front of you, feeling gratitude for the beauty around you. This daily practice will help you cultivate a more conscious presence and deeper appreciation for life's ephemeral moments.

MARCH 31–APRIL 4

THE SOUND OF DISTANT THUNDER

雷乃発声 *Kaminari sunawachi koe o hassu*

Just as distant thunder heralds the rebirth of nature, so every echo of change in our lives invites us to awaken new forces within us and renew ourselves with courage.

We now reach a phase that marks a time of transition in the traditional Japanese calendar. The thunder, with its portentous and distant echo, heralds the arrival of new energies and the renewal of life. This awakening makes us reflect on our personal renewal. What parts of you are ready to awaken? What new energies are ready to emerge in your life?

Thunder is also a symbol of our inner strength, a reminder to recognize and embrace our power. Although thunder is an external phenomenon, it can resonate with our inner storms, reminding us that we have the strength to face challenges. Thunder heralds a change in the weather, bringing rain and nourishment for the earth. Thus, changes in our lives, even those that may worry us, bring with them the opportunity for growth. This encourages us to see beyond the emotional turmoil and recognize potential blessings disguised as challenges. Thunder also invites us to listen. At this time, let us dedicate ourselves to listening attentively, not only to external sounds, but also to internal voices. What messages is our deeper self trying to convey to us? Is there perhaps an intuition or desire that has been dormant and is now, like the thunder, trying to make itself heard?

INNER THUNDER MEDITATION Use the powerful idea of thunder to help you navigate a time of change and use this as an opportunity for personal growth.

1. Find a quiet place where you will not be disturbed. Sit down and close your eyes. Take a few deep breaths to relax.
2. Imagine you are in a natural landscape, a field or forest. The sky darkens, heralding the arrival of a distant thunderstorm. You hear the sound of thunder in the distance, powerful and reverberating but not threatening.
3. As you listen to the thunder, bring your attention to your inner thunder. It represents your strength, aspirations, and approaching change. Listen without judgment, welcoming the feelings or emotions that have emerged.
4. Reflect on how this inner thunder invites you to change or grow. What is it trying to tell you? What parts of you are now ready for renewal?
5. It is now time to commit to change. Visualize yourself welcoming this change or growth.
6. When you feel ready, bring your attention to the present. Wiggle your fingers and toes, breathe deeply, and open your eyes.
7. If you wish, write down your reflections or the steps you plan to take in a journal.

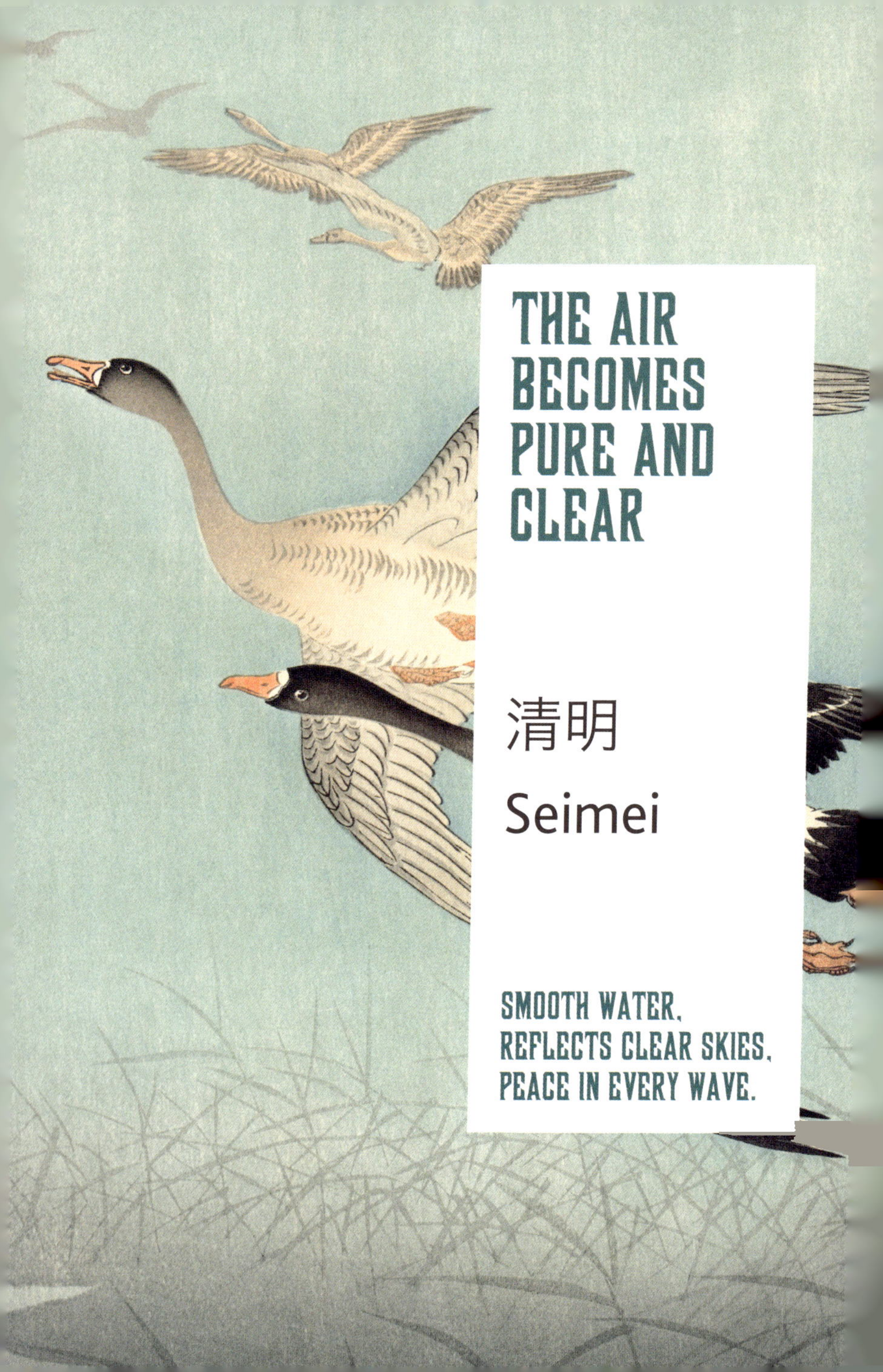

THE AIR BECOMES PURE AND CLEAR

清明

Seimei

SMOOTH WATER,
REFLECTS CLEAR SKIES,
PEACE IN EVERY WAVE.

APRIL 5–9

THE RETURN OF THE SWALLOWS

玄鳥至 *Tsubame kitaru*

No matter how long or hard the winter you have experienced, spring will always come, bringing with it new life and endless opportunities for rebirth.

The migration of swallows is a fascinating phenomenon that symbolizes not only the changing seasons, but also the incredible capacity for adaptation and resilience found in the natural world. These small but tenacious birds travel thousands of miles, crossing continents and oceans, to reach their nesting destinations, guided by deep instinct and amazing navigational skills. Their determination to overcome obstacles, such as adverse weather conditions and lack of rest, is a great metaphor: just like swallows, humans possess an innate ability to face and overcome challenges.

Resilience means not only enduring adversity, but being able to emerge from these experiences stronger, wiser, and with more flexibility. It also means being able to change course when necessary, accepting new circumstances, and finding innovative ways to deal with challenges.

Maintaining hope and a positive attitude, even in the most difficult times, provides us with the strength to keep fighting and looking for solutions; helps us see the opportunities hidden in the difficulties; and helps us believe in the possibility of a better future. Finally, resilience involves continuous growth: each challenge overcome makes us stronger and wiser. Acknowledging and celebrating our successes, no matter how small, fuels our self-esteem.

In a rapidly changing world, then, our ability to adapt and remain open to new ways of thinking and acting is crucial. Beware: adapting to the world and change does not mean giving up our values, but rather being flexible, and regarding change as opportunity.

The swallows' journey can also be seen as a metaphor for soul-searching. Each migration symbolizes the journeys we undertake in life.

THE FLIGHT OF THE SWALLOW This exercise will help you reflect on your adaptability and personal resilience.

1. Find a quiet place to sit, close your eyes, and take a few deep breaths, letting any tension melt away.
2. Imagine you are a swallow at the beginning of its migratory journey. Feel the determination and instinct guiding your flight through different routes, overcoming natural obstacles such as storms and headwinds. As you continue your journey, reflect on how you adapt to changes and challenges. What strategies do you use to navigate uncertainties? Acknowledge the strength and resilience you have shown in times of difficulty. Like the swallow, you have the skills to overcome adversity.
3. When you feel ready, bring your attention back to the present, moving your hands and feet, and finally opening your eyes.
4. Write your reflections in a journal.

APRIL 10–14

THE MIGRATION OF THE WILD GEESE

鴻雁北 *Kōgan kaeru*

As the wild geese soar over new lands, so we rise above challenges, guided by the strength of our vision and the community that flies with us.

The journey of the wild geese as a group heading north embodies the concepts of unity, collective resilience, and determination to achieve a common goal. Their migration is not just an instinctive act but an evolutionary strategy that maximizes the chances of success through the power of collaboration and the strength of pursuing a shared direction together.

The "V" formation of geese during flight is a lesson in natural physics applied to teamwork. Each bird, by beating its wings, creates an air lift for the bird behind it, thus reducing air resistance. This allows the group to fly for longer, using less energy than a single bird flying alone. This natural strategy teaches us that when we work together, supporting each other, we achieve goals that alone would be out of reach, thereby optimizing our resources.

The collective flight of wild geese also symbolizes the power of mutual support. On the long journey north, if one goose gets tired or sick, others will break away from the formation to follow it and protect it until it is ready to take flight again. This altruistic behavior recognizes that the strength of the group lies in the well-being of each individual member.

The migration of geese to distant lands also emphasizes the importance of having clear and shared goals within a community or team. Each spring, these birds embark on a journey back to their nesting sites, guided by an internal compass that directs them north. The journey of wild geese makes us reflect on our personal and collective journeys. It reminds us that we are not alone; community and collaboration can offer support, strength, and a shared direction toward our personal and collective "north."

YOUR "V" FLIGHT Taking the strategy of the wild geese as inspiration, meditate on your goals and ambitions and how the power of mutual support can assist you in your endeavors.

1. Take a moment to quieten your mind. Take a few deep breaths or meditate briefly to center yourself.
2. Reflect on the direction of your life at the current moment. What is your north? Write about the goals or dreams you are pursuing. Consider the people in your life who are part of your "V" formation. Who are your supporters? How do you support each other in achieving common goals?

3. Reflect on a time when you received support from others on your journey. How did that make you feel?
4. Think of an occasion when you offered support to someone. What was your role in their journey? How did you feel when you provided that support?
5. Take time to reflect on and share your answers and reflections.

APRIL 15–19

THE FIRST RAINBOWS APPEAR

虹始見 *Niji hajimete arawaru*

Every rainbow begins with rain; remember that even after the darkest times, beauty and hope can emerge, brightening the sky of your life.

The appearance of the first rainbows represents a moment of magical transition and the passage from storm to calm, from rain to light. Rainbows would not exist without rain, and those colors of rain are an invitation to recognize and accept challenges as an integral part of our growth, and to reveal those parts of ourselves that would otherwise remain hidden.

The rainbow, emerging from the meeting of rain and sunshine, symbolizes the process of integrating opposites. In this sense, the rainbow suggests that complete realization is possible only through the acceptance and integration of the different parts of self, both positive and negative.

According to Jung, the shadow represents those parts of ourselves hidden from our consciousness, often because they are at odds with the image we wish to project. These parts may include personality traits, desires, and memories that we consider negative or undesirable. This process of integration involves recognizing and accepting our hidden or "shadow" parts. This means facing our fears, uncertainties, and feelings of inadequacy, rather than repressing or ignoring them. The rainbow teaches us to embrace the totality of our experience, both light and shadow.

The appearance of a rainbow is also a visual reminder that the storm has passed and a new beginning is possible. It encourages us to maintain hope and is an especially powerful vision when we find ourselves stuck in negative thought cycles. Each rainbow encourages us to look for and recognize the light and color that live within us even when we feel suppressed by life's rains.

RAINBOW JOURNALING The next exercise reinforces resilience and hope through reflective writing, recognizing and celebrating moments of positive transformation in your life.

1 First, you will need a notebook or tablet where you capture the moments of beauty, hope, and growth that emerge from challenges. This will become your rainbow journal.

2 Each day, for a period of at least two weeks, set aside a few minutes to reflect on your daily experiences and identify at least one "rainbow"—a moment, a thought, an encounter, or anything that brought you a sense of hope.

3 Describe the event, and also how it made you feel and why you consider it a rainbow. In addition to daily rainbows, try reflecting on a more significant rainbow you have experienced in the past. This can be a period of difficulty that you overcame, a change that led to personal growth, or any experience that you feel contributed to your development.

4 This rewarding exercise will help you identify and appreciate the small joys in your life and recognize your path to growth and resilience. Through writing, you can give shape and meaning to your experiences, turning reflection into a daily practice of hope and gratitude.

RAINS FOR A GROWING HARVEST

穀雨

Kokuu

GREEN SWAYS THE FIELD,
HOPE AMONG THE BLADES
OF GRASS.
PROMISE OF BREAD.

APRIL 20–24

THE REEDS BEGIN TO SPROUT

葭始生 *Ashi hajimete shōzu*

Like the first reeds that sprout tenaciously from the earth, we too can emerge with strength and grace from the driest soils of our lives.

Reeds, with their remarkable ability to emerge from soils that may appear barren or inhospitable, offer a rich metaphor for resilience and regeneration. This process of growth and rebirth of reeds begins with their robust rhizomes, horizontal roots capable of surviving below the soil surface. During dormant periods, these rhizomes conserve vital energy and nutrients, waiting for the right time to sprout.

When spring arrives, warmer temperatures signal to the rhizomes that it is time to awaken. In response, the rhizomes begin to produce new shoots that push their way to the surface. The shoots are surprisingly strong and can penetrate hard, compacted soil. As they emerge, they turn into green, flexible plants, ready to grow tall and expand rapidly. The ability of reeds to emerge in a wide range of environments, including wet, swampy, or even polluted ones, testifies to their incredible adaptability and resilience. They effectively utilize places that other organisms might find inhospitable, transforming unfavorable environments into lush habitats.

Just as the rhizomes of the reeds preserve the resources needed for future growth, we too possess internal resources to draw on in times of need. And just as reed shoots make their way through the soil, we too can overcome obstacles and adversity, emerging stronger and regenerated.

THE GARDEN OF RESILIENCE Create a garden of resilience that will provide a safe place and offer encouragement in times of adversity.

1 Choose some plants that symbolize resilience and the capacity for regeneration to you. Reeds are just one example; you can choose any plant that conveys the idea of strength and flexibility. Take time to prepare the soil where you will put your plants. This act of care and preparation represents the inner work necessary to overcome adversity. While you work the soil, reflect on how you prepare yourself to face and overcome challenges in your life.

2 As you arrange your plants in the prepared soil, consider each one as a goal or an attribute of resilience that you wish to cultivate in yourself.

3 Gardening requires constant care, just like the process of personal growth. Take time to water, prune, and care for your resilience garden. This regular maintenance symbolizes ongoing commitment to your own development and well-being. Take a moment to observe your garden and reflect on the progress of the plants. Each new leaf, flower, or shoot can serve as a reminder of your ability to overcome adversity and regenerate.

4 Over time, your garden of resilience will become a place of refuge and inspiration, reminding you of your ability to grow and thrive, despite adversity.

APRIL 25–29

LAST FROST, RICE SEEDLINGS GROW

霜止出苗 *Shimo yamite nae izuru*

Even after the darkest moments, there is always room for a new beginning full of potential and hope.

The concept of growth and rebirth, inspired by the rice seedlings emerging after the last frost, is a metaphor for our ability to face and transcend adversity.

Time is a crucial factor in the growth cycle. Just as the rice seedlings do not emerge immediately after the last cold snap, but require patience and favorable conditions to develop, so the path of our personal growth also requires time and care. Patience teaches us to wait calmly for the fruits of our labor, while determination urges us to keep nurturing our dreams and aspirations, even when progress seems slow or invisible.

Finally, the concept of growth and rebirth emphasizes the importance of nurturing ourselves, both physically and emotionally. Just as rice seedlings need water, sunlight, and nutrients to flourish, so we must take care of our own well-being, feeding our body, mind, and spirit with that which fortifies and renews them.

We will then be able to see our challenges not as insurmountable obstacles, but as stages in our journey of growth, reminding ourselves that after every winter there is always spring.

THE PATH OF RESILIENCE This exercise transforms physical action into a reflective and symbolic practice, linking each step to the ability to move forward in life, overcome obstacles, and grow through challenges, so we can continue to move toward our rebirth and regeneration.

1. Choose a path to represent your resilience journey. It can be a path in the park, a local street, or even a path drawn on paper if you cannot get outside. If possible, include elements that symbolize challenges overcome or goals achieved, such as a climb to represent an obstacle or a viewpoint for an achievement.
2. Before you begin your journey, take a moment to reflect on the challenges you have faced in your life and how you were able to overcome them. Think about how each step you take can symbolize a step forward in your growth.

3. Begin your journey with the intention of leaving difficulties behind and moving toward new opportunities for growth. With each step, remind yourself of your strength and resilience.
4. At the end of the journey, set aside time to reflect on the experience. Think about how you felt along the way, any thoughts or emotions that surfaced, and how you can apply this feeling of progress to your daily life.
5. Consider keeping a journal of your resilience walk. Write down notable reflections gained during the walk and any ideas on how you can continue to build your resilience.

APRIL 30–MAY 4

PEONIES START TO BLOOM

牡丹華 *Botan hana saku*

Like the peonies that bloom with boldness, let us remember to bloom with grace and strength despite adversity.

The magnificent blooms of peonies, with their variety of vibrant colors and impressive shapes, embody the importance of patience and the beauty of waiting. Peonies may take years to develop their first buds, but once they bloom, they offer a spectacle that justifies the wait.

Once again, nature offers us a metaphor for human resilience and perseverance. In our journey, we often go through periods of preparation, during which it may seem that nothing is changing. However, just like peony buds, dreams and goals take time. The opening of peony buds reminds us that beauty can arise from situations that seem static and teaches us that perseverance and patience can turn into opportunities. The beauty of life often reveals itself in the most unexpected moments and ways.

CULTIVATING PATIENCE

Patience is a virtue that is often undervalued in our fast-paced world. In an age when everything is immediate, waiting is seen as a hindrance. However, peonies show us that true beauty and success are not instantaneous but take time to evolve.

Being patient does not mean developing the ability to wait, but learning to maintain a positive attitude while waiting. It is during these periods of stagnation that inner transformation takes place. Like peonies with their buds, we, too, develop our skills and resilience during periods of preparation, and cultivate a deeper understanding of ourselves and the world around us.

Waiting can be difficult and frustrating, but every moment is an opportunity to grow. The spectacular flowering of peonies is a reward for the patience and care invested in their development. Learning to be patient does not mean resigning oneself to inactivity, but rather accepting that progress takes time. During this process, we need to remain hopeful: we can engage in practices such as mindfulness, or set small to medium goals to make waiting more manageable.

Peonies remind us that patience is an essential ingredient for personal growth and fulfillment. Each stage of our journey, even the static ones, contributes to our eventual flourishing by showing us how to embrace patience and recognize the value of waiting.

THE PEONY JOURNAL This exercise invites you to keep a daily journal and jot down a beautiful thing you have noticed or experienced each day. It can be something simple, such as sharing a smile with a stranger or the taste of a meal cooked with love. The idea is to train the mind to recognize and appreciate these daily flowers in our lives. In time, this journal will become a reminder of the beauty you have noticed each day, encouraging you to remain patient and optimistic even during times of waiting.

THE BEGINNING OF SUMMER

立夏

Rikka

SUN HIGH AND STRONG,
PETALS DANCE PROUDLY,
SUMMER IS ANNOUNCED.

MAY 5–9

THE FROGS BEGIN TO CROAK

蛙始鳴 *Kawazu hajimete naku*

When frogs begin to croak, life echoes back in the quietest places, reminding us that every voice, even the smallest, has the power to awaken the world around it.

The croaking of frogs, resounding in the evenings of early May, marks not only the arrival of spring but also the awakening of nature after winter rest. This natural, life-filled song by frogs serves to attract partners, signal their presence in the territory, or alert others to potential dangers. Frog song is thus a means of establishing and maintaining connections within the species. Each sound contributes to a larger dialogue that sustains the social structure and survival of frogs in their community. Similarly, in human society, communication plays a key role in helping us to express our personal identity, build relationships, and define an individual's position. Just like frogs' singing, our communication can strengthen bonds, help us share vital information, and aid in the coordination of activities.

The croaking of frogs, then, invites us to consider our voices in the larger context of society, to reflect on how we use communication to influence and interact with the world around us. This allows us to explore not only how we speak, but also what we choose to say and how our messages can unite us. Moreover, the song of frogs, heard by many but fully understood only by individuals of that species, reminds us that every culture has its own unique language.

THE ART OF MINDFUL COMMUNICATION Use a conversation to practice mindful communication and afterward reflect on and learn from everything that was thought and said. Choose a conversation during which you will commit to being completely present. It can be a dialogue with a colleague, friend, or family member.

- **During the conversation**, if you notice that your attention begins to wander, bring it back to the present moment and focus on what the other person is saying.
- **Watch carefully** for the interlocutor's nonverbal characteristics, such as facial expressions, tone of voice, and gestures. This will help you stay anchored in the dialogue.
- **Pay attention** to how the other person reacts when they sense your full presence. Recognize any changes in his or her body language that indicate an appreciation for your attention.

After the conversation, take a moment to reflect.

- Who was your interlocutor? Describe the context of the conversation you've just had.
- What changes did you notice in the other person's behavior as a result of your active presence?
- Did you show signs of increased involvement or openness during the interchange? Where did your mind tend to wander during the conversation? What thoughts or concerns were distracting you?
- How did the person react to your renewed presence? Were there obvious signs, such as a smile or more eye contact, that indicated appreciation for your close attention?

MAY 10–14

EARTHWORMS EMERGE FROM THE GROUND

蚯蚓出 *Mimizu izuru*

From beneath the surface, every inner awakening brings with it a shoot of transformation; we embrace the process of emerging into the light to fully blossom.

The return of earthworms to the soil surface after a period spent deep underground is a symbol of renewal in nature. Worms play a crucial role in the ecosystem: they aerate the earth, decompose organic matter, and enrich the soil with nutrients, preparing the ground for new plant growth. The process of the worms' re-emergence can be likened to the inner journey that people take to face repressed or buried parts of themselves. This work is essential to our growth and well-being. Deep within ourselves, there may be thoughts, emotions, or past experiences that we have chosen to ignore or bury because they are difficult to deal with. Yet, just as earthworms rise to the surface and revitalize the soil, bringing these parts of ourselves to light can trigger a process of renewal. Recognizing these hidden aspects of ourselves allows us to address our personal history, to heal and grow. Our re-emergence may involve a period of discomfort or vulnerability. However, this process is necessary for long-term renewal. Facing what is hidden leads to greater self-understanding, resilience, and ultimately personal development.

LOOKING IN DEPTH The goal of this exercise is to use reflective writing to explore and better understand hidden aspects of the self, promoting a process of growth and awareness. Just like the worms that enrich the soil in silence, our inner work, though often not externally visible, is vital to our personal and emotional development.

1 Find a notebook or tablet and go to a quiet place, where you will not be disturbed and which makes you feel comfortable.

2. Begin by reflecting on an aspect of yourself or your life that you feel has remained hidden or not fully explored. It could be an undeveloped talent, a suppressed emotion, or a past experience that you never fully processed.
3. Write freely about this topic for 10–15 minutes, trying to understand why it has remained hidden and how it might affect your life if it were more out in the open.
4. Re-read what you have written and reflect on how these revelations can be integrated into your daily life to enhance your well-being or personal growth.
5. Write down some concrete steps you could take to address or further develop this aspect of yourself.

MAY 15–20

BAMBOO SHOOTS APPEAR

竹笋生 *Takenoko shōzu*

With the same invisible force that propels life toward the light, so too can we rise, transforming every obstacle into a step toward new heights.

The growth of bamboo is a unique process in the plant kingdom: this plant can grow up to 3 ft (90 cm) in a single day. However, what is special is its initial life cycle and the way it develops. Before the shoots emerge, bamboo spends years developing an extensive underground root system. These roots, invisible on the surface, support its vertical growth. Once the roots are well established, the stems (or culms) begin to emerge from the soil, growing at an astounding rate. This growth occurs in the rainy season, when moisture and temperature conditions are optimal. Bamboo culms can reach their full height in as little as 60–90 days, after which they transform from young and green to sturdy and woody.

The growth of bamboo is not just a miracle of speed and adaptability, but also a metaphor for change in humans. The way bamboo shoots adapt and grow under difficult conditions can be compared to our ability to adapt to the changing circumstances of life. This flexibility is not just a reaction to change, but a proactive adaptation too. Therefore, the way bamboo shoots emerge from darkness into light can serve as inspiration.

GUIDED MEDITATION: THE RESILIENCE OF BAMBOO Use the qualities of bamboo as the inspiration for this meditation on growth, resilience, and flexibility.

1. Choose a place where you will not be disturbed. You can sit in a chair with your feet planted on the floor or on a cushion in a meditation position. Make sure your back is straight but not stiff. Close your eyes. Breathe in and out. Each time you inhale, imagine you are bringing in clean, refreshing energy. When you exhale, let go of tensions and worries.
2. Imagine that you are a bamboo shoot, with deep roots extending into the fertile soil beneath you. They anchor you, providing the stability you need to grow. Feel connected to the earth, stable and secure.
3. Each day you become taller, stronger, and more flexible. With each breath you take, feel your spine lengthen toward the sky.
4. As the bamboo grows, it remains flexible, bending with the wind but not breaking. Reflect on how to incorporate this quality into your life.
5. Focus on the bamboo within you. Maintain this image of growth, flexibility, and strength. When you are ready, bring your attention back to the room. Keep this feeling of calm, resilience, and strength with you for the rest of the day.
6. Remember the lesson of the bamboo: even in times of great change, we can remain grounded, grow, and thrive.

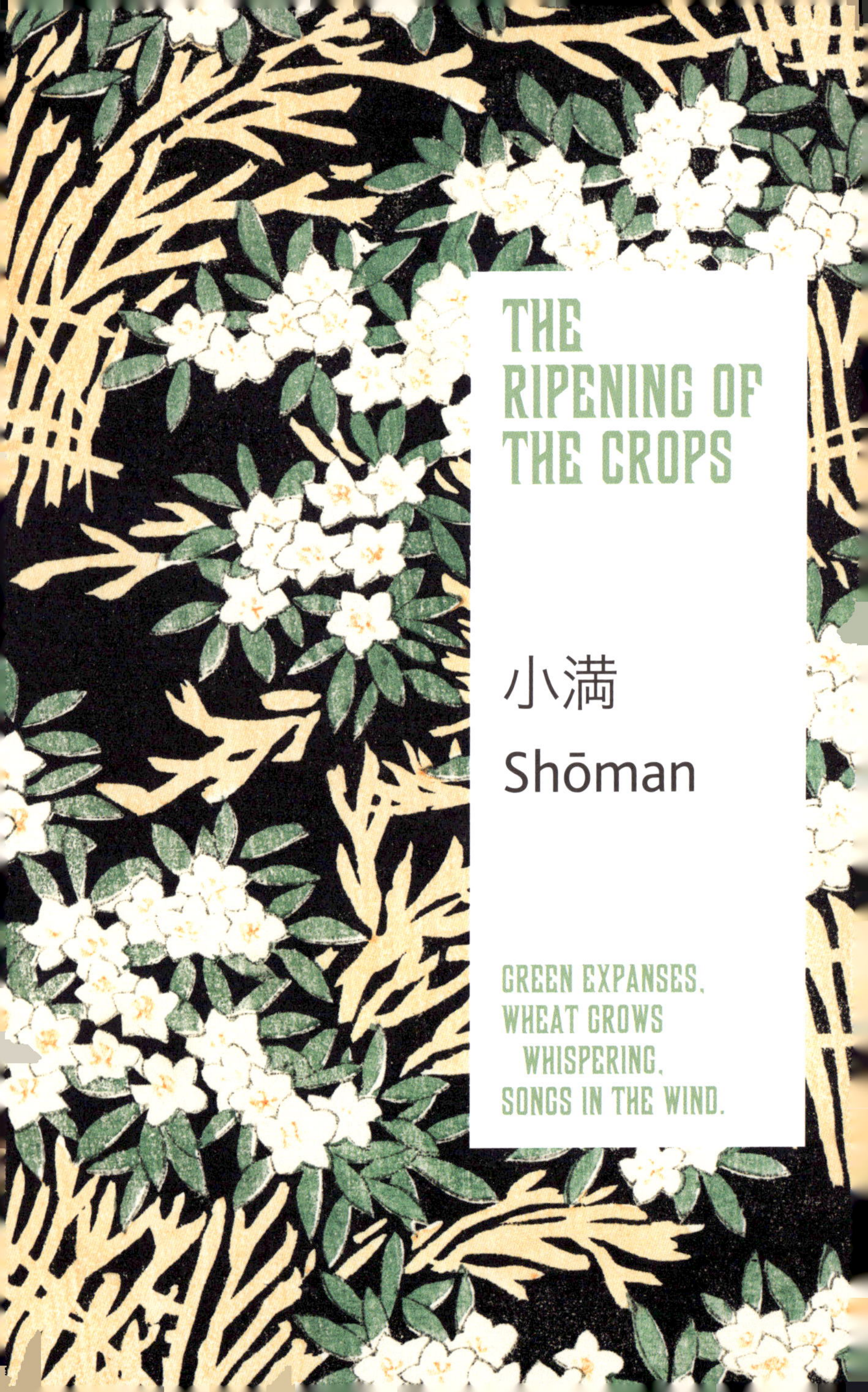

THE RIPENING OF THE CROPS

小満

Shōman

GREEN EXPANSES,
WHEAT GROWS
WHISPERING,
SONGS IN THE WIND.

MAY 21–25

SILKWORMS FEAST ON MULBERRY LEAVES

蚕起食桑 *Kaiko okite kuwa o hamu*

Just as silkworms feed on the mulberry leaves to transform, so we can feed mind and spirit to weave the patterns of our future.

The life cycle of silkworms, which use the nourishment from mulberry leaves to move from the larval to the butterfly stage, shows us how nourishment and development are interconnected. This metamorphosis transforms the caterpillars into creatures capable of flight and reproduction, bestowing life on new generations.

In the human context, each stage of our life journey requires different kinds of nourishment to sustain growth. In infancy, for example, we need physical nourishment for the proper development of the body, but also educational and effective stimuli to form the foundations of critical thinking and social skills. As we grow, needs change, and what we consume contributes to our development.

The silkworm metaphor teaches us to be aware of the type and amount of nourishment we introduce into our lives. This includes thinking critically about the media we consume, the company we keep, and the activities to which we devote our time. Each choice can contribute to our development.

In addition, just as silkworms have periods of apparent inactivity when they are in fact undergoing an intentional internal transformation, we too may need periods of internal reflection and renewal. These periods may seem unproductive from the outside. However, it is often during this time that the most significant transformations take shape.

The life cycle of silkworms is a reminder that adequate nourishment, both physical and psychological, is critical not only for maintenance but also for transformation.

RECIPES FOR PERSONAL GROWTH Keeping a journal of all the ingredients that support your personal and professional growth can help you identify new areas to explore and support future progress.

1. Find a notebook or tablet where you can note down your reflections. Think about the "foods" that currently support your personal and professional growth. These may include educational activities, personal relationships, hobbies, or spiritual practices.
2. Jot down these items in your journal. Reflect on how each of these elements affects your life. Write down your observations and feelings related to each element of nourishment. Consider what new foods you might introduce into your diet to encourage further growth and development. This might mean seeking new experiences, forming new relationships, or learning new skills. Set concrete goals for integrating these new elements into your life.
3. Set aside time regularly to revisit your journal and update your thoughts and plans. Evaluate progress and make adjustments if necessary.

MAY 26–30

THE SAFFLOWER BLOOMS

紅花栄 *Benibana sakau*

Like the vibrant blossoms of the safflower, we too can show our true nature, shining brightly and coloring the world with our uniqueness.

The safflower, characterized by its vivid red flowers, is a striking example of how aesthetics and utility can converge harmoniously. This eye-catching plant is also a source of valuable substances such as oil and dyes, with uses ranging from cooking to textile production.

The bright red safflower is traditionally associated with courage and strength. From a psychological point of view, its bloom represents an act of daring, an emergence from latency to full expression, a metamorphosis parallel to the human process of recognizing and manifesting one's inner potential. Revealing one's abilities and feelings to the world requires courage, especially when one exposes oneself to public judgment. When a person decides to openly express his or her talents or emotions, like the safflower exposing his or her flowers to the world, they are actively contributing to the life of their community. This contribution can take many forms: from cultural and artistic enrichment to solving practical problems. The manifestation of one's inner potential not only enriches one's life, but can also bring significant and beneficial changes to one's surroundings.

The blossoming of the safflower tells of the importance of an internal stage occurring before the results can be visible externally. Similarly, people go through a process of self-acceptance and recognition of their abilities before successfully manifesting them in the world. This internal development is crucial for confidence and self-esteem.

SELF-EXPRESSION THROUGH ART Choose an art that resonates with you, be it drawing, painting, writing, music, dance, or any form that allows you to express yourself freely.

1. Be inspired by safflower flowers and spend time creating something that expresses your individuality. It could be a work of art that uses red as the dominant color, a poem that explores themes of growth and courage, or a dance that expresses freedom and beauty.
2. Reflect on the creative process and how you felt during the act of creating. Consider what you discovered about yourself and what aspects of your personality emerged most clearly.

3. If you feel comfortable, share your work with others, either in an informal environment with friends or family, or in a more public showcase, such as a blog, art show, or exhibition.
4. Listen to feedback from those who see or experience your artwork, noting how external perceptions can provide additional insights into your self-expression.

MAY 31–JUNE 5

THE GRAIN RIPENS AND IS HARVESTED

麦秋至 *Mugi no toki itaru*

We cultivate our projects and passions with care and dedication, confident that every seed planted today will ripen into splendid achievements tomorrow.

Grain represents an essential component, not only of our diet, but also of Japanese culture. Although rice is considered the dominant grain, wheat is also used in the production of udon, soba, ramen, and various types of bread. In addition to its culinary importance, wheat also influences Japan's agricultural economy, with extensive cultivation contributing to the subsistence of rural communities. In this context, the wheat cycle is also deeply intertwined with the seasons and cultural practices, reflecting the rhythm of life.

The life cycle of wheat, extending from planting to final harvest, is an incisive metaphor for the path of personal and professional growth. In addition to being fundamental to food production, this agricultural process offers profound insights into how the stages of development and maturation can also be applied to human life.

Planting represents the phase of planning and beginning. In personal and professional growth, this stage corresponds to the setting of goals and the launching of new projects. Our projects require well-prepared ground.

After planting, the grain grows by going through several stages of development. At this stage, resilience is key, as challenges and unforeseen events can occur, just like adverse weather that affects wheat growth.

The ripening and harvesting of grain represents the culmination of the agricultural cycle, the time when the fruits of hard work become visible, and we can validate our methods.

CELEBRATING THE HARVEST The goal is to recognize and celebrate achievements in one's life projects, large or small. This exercise increases awareness of one's accomplishments and instills gratitude for our journey.

1. Find a quiet place and bring a journal with you to write down your thoughts.
2. Think about the investments you have made in yourself, your relationships, or your career over the past few months or years. These might include education, health, work projects, or personal development. Write down these investments and reflect on how they have matured over time.
3. For each investment, describe the results achieved. These may range from goals reached, lessons learned, or even just the satisfaction of the task completed. Evaluate how these results have affected your life and well-being.
4. Take a moment to celebrate these achievements. You may choose to share your accomplishments with friends or family, or simply give yourself a personal moment of gratitude.
5. Recognize the importance of each step in the process, from planting to harvesting, and thank yourself for your perseverance and hard work.

PLANTING THE GRAIN

芒種

Bōshu

LIGHT RAIN FALLS,
AMONG THE FRESHLY
TRACED FURROWS,
LIFE SPROUTS.

JUNE 6–10

PRAYING MANTISES HATCH FROM THEIR EGGS

蟷螂生 *Kamakiri shōzu*

In calmness lies strength; we learn to wait with serenity, knowing that the right moments will present themselves to reveal our full potential.

The hatching of praying mantises causes us to reflect on transformation and rebirth. These insects, known for their capacity to wait calmly and firmly before acting, offer a vivid representation of patience. Mantis behavior can be interpreted as a symbol of our ability to cope with life and adapt to change.

The process by which mantis nymphs hatch symbolizes a new beginning. Each new phase brings with it challenges and opportunities, and in nature the ability to adapt quickly is critical to success. Similarly, in our lives, emerging from difficult situations or periods of stalemate can be seen as an opportunity for rebirth and renewal.

The praying mantis is celebrated for its lethal precision and impeccable timing in seeking the right moment to strike its prey. This strategy of patience and calculation not only maximizes the chances of success but also reduces exposure to danger. This behavior can be applied metaphorically to human decisions, where timing and precision are often crucial. Rushed decisions can lead to mistakes and failures, while a thoughtful and measured approach can lead to much more satisfactory results.

Finally, the mantis passes through a period of development inside the egg, preparing for life outside. Preparing to face life's challenges through education, work experience, or self-improvement is crucial.

THE CALMNESS OF THE MANTIS This practice is inspired by the ability of praying mantises to remain still and calm before acting. The goal is to develop patience, improving the ability to respond to everyday situations.

1. Choose a place where you will not be disturbed. You can sit in a chair with your feet firmly planted on the floor, or on a cushion in a meditation position with your legs crossed. Make sure your back is straight but not stiff. Close your eyes. Breathe in and out slowly, allowing your body to relax.
2. Imagine you are a mantis, sitting still and calm, fully present in the moment. Focus on the rhythm of your breathing. Notice the cool air entering your nostrils, the lifting of your chest and abdomen, and then the soft release of air. If your mind begins to wander, bring your attention back to the breath, just as a mantis would bring its attention back to its surroundings.
3. Reflect on how patient the mantis must be and how crucial that patience is to its success. Reflect on how you might apply that same patience.
4. When you are ready, bring your attention to the present. After your meditation, describe your experiences in a journal.

JUNE 11–15

FIREFLIES RISE FROM ROTTING GRASS

腐草為螢 *Kusaretaru kusa hotaru to naru*

Even in the darkest of nights, remember that every star shines brightest when the sky is at its darkest point.

The emergence of fireflies from decaying grass is a potent symbol of how life can flourish even in conditions that would seem unpropitious. This natural phenomenon not only enchants with its beauty, but once again conveys a profound message about the resilience and potential for renewal we possess. Fireflies arise from a substrate of decay, transforming adversity into wonderful new life.

HUMAN RESILIENCE REFLECTED IN NATURE

The glowing fireflies transforming the dark night into a theater of dancing lights provide a metaphor for human resilience. This tells us that despite adverse circumstances, we have the innate ability to overcome them, adapting and transforming our negative experiences into sources of personal and collective growth.

BEAUTY AND HOPE IN DIFFICULT TIMES

Fireflies do not just survive; they thrive by transforming their environment into a light show, as do human beings who can find beauty and hope even in the darkest moments. This capacity is not only a question of survival, but also of healing and inspiration. Facing difficulties by actively seeking moments of beauty transforms challenges into opportunities for personal enlightenment and spiritual growth.

ILLUMINATING DARK MOMENTS WITH INNER STRENGTH AND CREATIVITY

The example of the fireflies invites us to consider how we can use our creativity to light up our lives and the lives of others. Every individual has a unique light, and in sharing this light we can inspire others and create brighter and more resilient communities.

Creativity is a powerful means of illuminating difficult moments and inspiring hope. This can be done by writing: keep a diary where you note down thoughts and feelings to help process your emotions and find a sense of clarity and relief. You can also write poems, stories, and letters to yourself to express your inner light. Alternatively, you can paint, draw, or create collages; art is a powerful tool for transforming negative emotions into visual expressions of beauty. Or, you can try composing music or playing an instrument as a way to connect with your emotions and with others.

You can also capture moments of beauty through the lens of a camera; photography can help you see the world with new eyes. Finally, cooking also expresses our creativity: preparing meals with love and attention to detail can be a form of creativity that nourishes not only the body but also the soul. Sharing food with others can help you create deep connections and bring joy.

Incorporating all these activities into daily life allows us to find moments of light even in the darkest days, emulating the dance of fireflies.

LIGHTING THE WAY The goal of this exercise is to use reflective writing to explore and transform difficult personal experiences into stories of growth and resilience, inspired by the life cycle of fireflies emerging luminous from the darkness. This exercise not only helps you process and recontextualize difficult experiences, but also promotes a proactive approach to future challenges, strengthening your ability to see and create beauty even in the darkest moments.

1 Begin by reflecting on recent or past events in your life that have challenged you or brought significant difficulties. It could be personal problems, professional problems, losses, failures, or any other experience that you consider a significant challenge.

2 Write in detail about these experiences, describing the emotions, thoughts, and reactions they aroused in you. Focus on describing not only the external events, but also your internal experience.

3 Now transform the narrative. Rewrite each experience with a new perspective; focus on how each difficulty led you to a form of personal growth, positive change, or new understanding. Try to identify the bright moments, those in which, despite the difficulty, something beautiful or useful emerged, just as fireflies emerge from decaying grass.

4 As you re-read what you have written, try to identify common themes of resilience and strength that run through your stories.

These can become the pillars of your understanding of how you face and overcome challenges.

5 If you feel comfortable, share some of these new stories with trusted friends or in a support group. Discussing and sharing these experiences can not only offer additional insights but also strengthen your sense of connection and support.

6 Finally, celebrate your journey of transformation. Recognize the courage, strength, and resilience you have shown in turning challenges into opportunities for growth, just as fireflies turn the night into a starry sky.

JUNE 16–20

PLUMS TURN YELLOW

梅子黄 *Ume no mi kibamu*

Time turns every challenge into a life lesson, teaching us to grasp the value of each moment with gratitude and deep understanding.

The yellowing and ripening of plums represents a crucial transition period, marking the transformation of these fruits from an unripe to a fully ripe state. In the same way that these fruits evolve over time under the influence of specific environmental factors, so individuals also go through stages of ripening that are the result of their experiences and the context in which they live.

Plums do not ripen suddenly; they require time and favorable environmental conditions. Similarly, personal growth and emotional development need long periods and often appropriate conditions for potential to be fully realized. Life challenges and experiences for us are like nutrients and sunshine for plums: they are essential to the developmental process.

GROWING THROUGH CHALLENGES

In the same way that plums cope with summer heat and mature through environmental difficulties, so do people often draw the greatest lessons from times of challenge and pressure. In this sense, overcoming difficulties can be likened to the assimilation of essential nutrients that are crucial to the process of personal growth, in a similar way to the elements that influence the ripening of plums.

LESSONS AND OPPORTUNITIES IN EVERY SEASON OF LIFE

Each stage of life brings unique lessons and opportunities for growth, just as each season contributes differently to the life cycle of a plum. Recognizing and accepting that each period of our existence has intrinsic value can help us live it more fully.

During childhood, learning and play experiences are crucial. Just like plums beginning to develop from buds, children absorb early life lessons, developing the foundations of character and social skills. Growing up as adolescents they face the pressures of studies, personal relationships, peer pressure, and life choices, maturing through each experience. This stage is comparable to summer for plums, when heat and environmental challenges promote growth. Adulthood, on the other hand, represents the time when plums reach full maturity. Work, family, and personal responsibilities require the application of lessons learned in the preceding stages. As with ripe plums, old age represents a time for reflection and harvesting the fruits of a life's work. Older people share their wisdom and experiences with younger generations, thus completing the life cycle.

Each stage of life has its own unique value and important lessons. Just as plums go through various stages of development until they reach their full maturity, we too can grow and develop through the experiences of our lives. Let us embrace each moment with gratitude, knowing that each challenge and success brings us closer to our complete personal fulfillment.

LIFE LESSONS The goal of this exercise is to explore your personal journey toward maturity, identifying the lessons learned and evaluating how they contributed to your growth. This exercise not only helps you value your personal journey of maturation but also promotes a reflective approach toward self-understanding, stimulating gratitude for your experiences and how they have helped to shape your identity and wisdom.

1. Take a moment to reflect on the various stages of your life, such as childhood, adolescence, and adulthood. Note down significant experiences that you believe have contributed to your personal growth.
2. For each experience, reflect on how it influenced your perception, behavior, and decisions. Try to identify specific life lessons you learned and how these shaped the person you are today.
3. Consider how you have changed over the years. What were the turning points? How have you handled challenges and changes? Reflect on how your ability to manage emotions and relationships has evolved.
4. If you feel comfortable, share some of your reflections with a person you trust. Discussing your experiences and lessons learned can offer new perspectives and further insights.
5. Recognize and celebrate your journey of growth and maturation. Appreciate the efforts you have made to overcome challenges and adversity—just like plums that, season after season, ripen to their full potential.

THE SUMMER SOLSTICE

夏至

Geshi

THE SKY SHINES,
SHADOWS RETREAT
AT NOON,
HEAT EMBRACES
EVERYTHING.

JUNE 21–26

THE SELF-HEAL WILTS

乃東枯 *Natsukarekusa karuru*

Every conclusion carries with it the seed of a new beginning, with shoots ready to appear when the time is ripe.

The wilting flowers of Asian self-heal (*Prunella vulgaris* subsp. *asiatica*), a phenomenon intrinsic to its life cycle, embody the principle of transience in nature, underscoring how change is a universal law from which nothing and no one can escape. Watching the decline of the self-heal flowers reminds us that every conclusion is a prelude to a new beginning, and that the cycles of life, death, and rebirth are interconnected and essential to continuous renewal.

In addition, this awareness can lead to a greater acceptance of stages of decline or end. Psychologically, this can translate into a greater ability to handle loss and change, finding serenity in the inevitability of these events. Being aware of the impermanence of existence teaches us that every phase of life brings with it both beauty and purpose, even those that may seem less desirable or more difficult to accept. The ability to let go of old habits, convictions, relationships, or situations that no longer serve our well-being or growth, symbolized by the falling petals, is essential to the continuous cycle of renewal. Ultimately, the wilting of self-heal is not only a symbol of the end, but also a reminder of the perpetual rebirth and continuity of life. This lesson invites us to reflect on our reactions to change, encouraging us to accept and appreciate the mysterious and wonderful cycle of life.

CYCLES OF LIFE Here the goal is to reflect on the cyclical nature of life, developing acceptance of the stages of its conclusion, and preparing for new beginnings.

1. Spend time reflecting on a phase of your life that has come to an end or is coming to an end. Write down in your journal your thoughts and feelings. Explore what you learned from the experience and how it changed you.
2. Create a small detachment ritual to symbolize the end of this phase. This might include writing a letter you won't send, planting something in your garden, or even just taking a walk.
3. Think about what you would like to see happen next. What are your hopes and plans for the next chapter of your life? Write down these thoughts.
4. Conclude the exercise by acknowledging and celebrating the beauty and teachings that each stage of life brings. Be grateful for past experiences and remain open and optimistic about future possibilities.

JUNE 27–JULY 1

THE IRISES BLOOM

菖蒲華 *Ayame hana saku*

Like the irises that bloom with elegance, we can bloom in our uniqueness, showing the world the beauty of our true nature.

The Japanese water iris (*Iris ensata*) has deep roots in Japanese culture. First selectively bred during the Edo period (1603–1868) there are now more than 2,000 varieties of this plant.

Known for its large, colorful flowers, ranging from blue to white through shades of lavender and pink, the Japanese water iris is not only admired for its beauty, but is also loaded with meaning: blue iris is commonly associated with optimism and faith, while purple iris represents knowledge and dignity. These flowers are also seen as symbols of courage, health, hope, and protection. Traditionally, they are believed to drive away evil spirits and protect against negative influences. Every year on Children's Day (*Kodomo No Hi*), iris leaves are used in baths for children to wish them strength and protection.

LESSONS FROM THE JAPANESE IRIS

Rich in symbolism from a historical and cultural perspective, this flower offers valuable lessons that can be applied to daily life. It represents not only beauty and elegance, but also deeper concepts such as strength, protection, and the ability to renew oneself.

Resilience with elegance: The iris teaches us that it is possible to face adversity and challenges while maintaining one's integrity and dignity. The ability of the iris to remain strong and flexible in the face of life's storms symbolizes resilience. The iris reminds us that true strength lies not in rigidity, but in the ability to adapt and thrive.

Purification and protection: Long associated with purification and spiritual protection, the iris suggests the importance of surrounding ourselves with an environment that promotes our mental and emotional health. In the same way that the iris is said to repel evil spirits, so we can learn to protect ourselves from negative influences by creating spaces that support tranquility and peace.

Acceptance of change: The iris blooms in a cycle of continuous renewal, a powerful reminder that change is a natural and inevitable part of life. This flower teaches us to see change not as a threat, but as an opportunity. An attitude of openness can lead to meaningful personal discoveries and a strengthening of one's sense of self.

Growth through change: Finally, the blooming of irises symbolizes the transformation and beauty that can emerge through change. It encourages us not to fear uncertainty, but to embrace it as a passage to new stages of personal development. Each bloom represents the possibility of reinvention and expressing new versions of oneself.

GUIDED MEDITATION ON THE IRIS GARDEN The goal of this exercise is to meditate on the inherent qualities of the iris and develop them within yourself. This meditation aims to strengthen your inner connection with the qualities of resilience, beauty, and transformation represented by the iris, helping you to rediscover your capacity for personal renewal and inner growth.

1. Find a quiet place where you can sit or lie down comfortably. Make sure you are not disturbed during your meditation. You can listen to background music if it helps you relax.
2. Sit or lie down in a comfortable position. Close your eyes and take three deep breaths. With each exhalation, feel your body relax, letting all your tension slowly melt away.
3. Imagine that roots are growing from the base of your spine, extending deep into the earth. Feel the stability and nourishment that comes from this connection to the soil. Absorb this energy of stability and calm.
4. Visualize a beautiful garden of irises in full bloom. Each flower is vibrant and full of life. Mentally walk through this garden, noticing the details of each flower you encounter: the colors, the forms, and the way they move slightly with the breeze.
5. Approach an iris that particularly catches your eye. Sit beside it and focus on it intently, trying to glean its intrinsic qualities as well as its beauty.
6. As you observe the flower, reflect on how you, too, are continually growing and transforming. Consider the challenges you have faced and how these have allowed you to grow and flourish, just like the iris.
7. Breathe in the qualities of the iris: beauty, strength, and resilience. With each inhalation, feel these qualities fill your being. With each exhalation, let go of your fears, doubts, and uncertainties.

8. Spend a few moments in silence, allowing yourself to absorb the peace and tranquility of the garden. Feel renewed and revitalized by this exercise.
9. When you are ready, slowly bring your attention to gratitude for this experience of connecting with nature and the symbolic significance of the iris. Recognize the continuous cycle of growth and rebirth in your life.
10. When you feel the meditation is complete, slowly bring your attention to the present. Gently move your fingers and toes, and when you feel ready, open your eyes.
11. Take a moment to note down any thoughts or insights that came to you during this meditation, so you can reflect on them later.

JULY 2–6

THE SHOOTS OF BAN XIA APPEAR

半夏生 *Hange shōzu*

Times of difficulty are the most fertile soil for planting the seed of our personal development.

Ban xia or the crow-dipper (*Pinellia ternata*) is a perennial plant native to China and Japan. The shoots of the crow-dipper embody rebirth and hidden potential. The ability of this plant to sprout from the soil, often under adverse conditions, is a living expression of its strength. The way this plant makes its way through the soil to reach for light and air can serve as a powerful metaphor for our own personal journey as we overcome life's obstacles.

Each of us possesses hidden potential just waiting to be brought to light. Like the seeds of the crow-dipper, we have internal resources not yet manifested that are just waiting for the right conditions to emerge and flourish. This process of discovering our potential can be catalyzed by challenges and changes, prompting us to explore new possibilities and reinvent ourselves. This plant is a reminder that, despite adversity, we can emerge stronger, wiser, and more capable. It also teaches us that, beyond external conditions, the potential for renewal and growth always exists within us.

RECOGNIZE AND NURTURE YOUR INNER POTENTIAL Here the goal is to develop awareness of one's potential for growth and renewal through reflection and creative visualization.

1. Begin by thinking back to a time in your life when you felt that you were coming into bud after a quiet or difficult phase. Record this time in your journal, describing the challenges you faced.
2. Sit in a quiet place and close your eyes. Imagine you are a plant beginning to sprout. Visualize your roots reaching deep into the earth, absorbing nutrients. Your inner strength drives you to grow toward the sunlight, despite the layers of soil.
3. Reflect on internal and external resources that have helped, or can help you to grow—personal qualities such as determination or creativity, support from your friends and family, or professional skills.
4. List specific ways in which you can nurture and support your personal growth over the coming months. Set small goals that will enable you to continue to grow and develop to your full potential.
5. Conclude the exercise by expressing gratitude for your path of growth and for the resources you have available to you. Remind yourself that, like the crow-dipper, you have the inner strength to overcome challenges and flourish.

THE SUN'S RAYS WARM THE EARTH

小暑

Shōsho

WARM WIND,
SHADOWS LENGTHEN,
SUMMER BURNS.

JULY 7–11

THE SUMMER WIND BLOWS

温風至 *Atsukaze itaru*

Let change propel you like the summer wind toward new horizons, allowing you to fly higher than you ever imagined.

At the beginning of July, Japan witnesses the arrival of warm winds that mark the gradual move into summer. This phenomenon coincides with periods of celebration and rituals, such as *Tanabata*, the festival of stars, held on July 7. During *Tanabata*, people write their wishes on *tanzaku*, small strips of paper, and hang them on bamboo branches, hoping that the winds will carry their wishes into the sky. This festival symbolizes hope and aspiration, foundational elements in Japan's cultural fabric, and reflects the connection between natural events and human life.

Welcoming these winds as harbingers of new beginnings and possibilities, we gain inspiration to renew our lives: just as summer winds transform the landscape, we too can use periods of change to open our minds to new ideas and opportunities. Summer winds renew the energy of nature, and we can also infuse new energy into our projects. This is also an ideal time for reflection, assessing our progress and planning for the future. Summer winds remind us that in spite of challenges, there is always the chance for rebirth and growth.

TANABATA You can also perform the ritual associated with *Tanabata*, committing your wishes to paper, so they can drive you forward in life.

1 Find a quiet place to sit. Gather some sheets of colored paper, a pen, and a small branch or board where you can hang or pin your wishes for the future.

2 Close your eyes and take a few deep breaths to center yourself. Imagine a clear, starry night sky above you. Feel the connection

between yourself and the Universe and open your heart to the deepest desires you want to express.

3. Open your eyes and write your wishes or goals on strips of colored paper.
4. For each wish, reflect on steps you can take to get closer to its fulfillment. Note these steps on the back of the strip.
5. Hang the strips from the branch or pin them to the board, so you will see them regularly.
6. Spend a few minutes visualizing the fulfillment of each wish. Imagine how you will feel when these wishes become reality.
7. Thank the Universe for making your wishes come true and don't forget to regularly review your progress toward their fulfillment.

July 12–16

THE FIRST LOTUS FLOWERS BLOOM

蓮始開 *Hasu hajimete hiraku*

It is not the purity of circumstances, but the strength of your spirit that determines your ability to shine.

The lotus flower (*Nelumbo nucifera*) is deeply rooted in the culture and spiritual traditions of Japan. It blooms in calm, marshy waters and is

known for its ability to emerge clean and perfect from the mud at the bottom of the pond. This unique characteristic not only makes it an emblem of purity and beauty, but also of rebirth and spiritual awakening.

The lotus is often associated with the Buddha figure, symbolizing spiritual enlightenment. According to some legends, wherever the Buddha laid his feet as a child, a lotus flower grew. Moreover, the *Lotus Sutra* is one of the most important texts in Mahayana Buddhism. Its story suggests to us that true beauty emerges despite humble origins or a difficult background.

The resilience of the lotus also resonates with the Japanese philosophy of overcoming difficulties with grace. This flower represents the ability to remain calm even in the most difficult situations, a principle that aligns with Zen teachings such as overcoming earthly attachments and the pursuit of inner peace. In the cultural context of Japan, the lotus also symbolizes regeneration and immortality, often found in stories and works of art that explore themes of life, death, and rebirth. Its presence in gardens and temples is not only decorative but also a constant reminder to reflect and meditate.

GROWTH AND REBIRTH

The life cycle of the lotus, which comes out of the mud to emerge immaculately on the surface of the water, teaches us that no matter how difficult or dirty our origins or circumstances may be, we have the ability to overcome them and be reborn into higher, purified forms. This is a lesson that encourages the individual not to let their difficulties define them.

PURITY AND INTEGRITY

The lotus blooms with a beauty untouched by the muddy environment from which it came. This characteristic can be interpreted as a call to maintain purity and clarity of purpose and values, despite external challenges. The ability to maintain one's integrity in adverse situations can be cultivated through the practice of mindfulness and self-reflection.

RESILIENCE AND ADAPTABILITY

This flower reminds us that resilience is not a static trait and that we can develop it by responding positively to stress and adversity. The example of the lotus flower encourages us to find creative and adaptive ways to overcome obstacles.

ENLIGHTENMENT AND SPIRITUAL AWAKENING

In the Buddhist context, the lotus is often associated with the path to enlightenment. Each petal of the lotus can represent a step along the spiritual path, culminating in the full bloom that symbolizes awakening. This invites us to consider our path of spiritual and personal growth as a gradual process that requires patience, commitment, and dedication.

The lessons of the lotus flower urge us to improve our present condition, but also to strive for continuous renewal, to awaken our potential, and to pay attention to purity of spirit.

LOTUS FLOWER MEDITATION The goal of this exercise is to meditate on the qualities of the lotus flower to develop purity, peace, resilience, and wisdom. The meditation can be practiced regularly to strengthen these qualities, helping you to live with greater intention and harmony.

1. Choose a quiet, comfortable place where you will not be disturbed. Make sure to have a comfortable seat and, if you wish, play gentle sounds such as the sound of water or meditative music in the background.
2. Sit in a comfortable position with your back straight and close your eyes. Take a few deep breaths, inhaling slowly through your nose and exhaling through your mouth. With each exhalation, release tension and worries, allowing your body to unwind and relax completely.

3. Imagine that from the base of your spine, there are roots extending deep into the ground, anchoring you firmly to the earth. Feel the solidity of the ground beneath you and the calmness this connection brings.
4. In your mind, visualize a calm, still pond. In the center of the pond imagine a lotus bud that is about to open. Observe the mud around the bud; this represents the challenges and difficulties you have faced.
5. As you continue to breathe deeply, watch the lotus bud slowly begin to open and unfurl, emerging from the mud. With each breath, the flower opens gradually, showing its immaculately clean petals despite its muddy origins. Each unfurling petal represents a quality you wish to develop, be that purity, peace, resilience, or wisdom.
6. Now that the lotus flower is fully open, imagine its purity and beauty radiating from the petals and enveloping you. Feel these qualities entering your body with every breath, infusing each cell with serenity and strength. Allow these sensations to dissolve any negativity or doubt, leaving only clarity and calm.
7. Reflect on how you can bring the qualities of the lotus flower into your daily life. Think about specific actions or attitude changes that will help you manifest these qualities. Set an intention to maintain this connection to the purity and resilience of the lotus.
8. When you feel ready, slowly begin to bring your awareness back to the present. Gently move your fingers and toes, and when you feel completely present, open your eyes.
9. Conclude the meditation by expressing gratitude for the lessons learned from the lotus flower and for the time you have devoted to this practice of inner growth.

JULY 17–22

THE HAWKS LEARN TO FLY

鷹乃学習 *Taka sunawachi waza o narau*

Embrace the wind of challenges like the hawk; it is only by opening our wings to the storm that we can rise to new heights and realize our full potential.

Hawks are members of the bird family Accipitridae. Hawks are known for their extraordinary flying ability and skills as a predator. In Japan, the hawk (*taka* たか) is historically revered as a symbol of boldness and virility. Falconry was an aristocratic pastime, particularly favored by the samurai class, which held political power from 1185–68. The warriors identified themselves with these creatures for their nobility, ferocity, and ability to undergo the discipline of domestication. The hawk's keen eyesight, predatory nature, and courage reflected the ideal qualities of the warrior, making these birds a powerful symbol of martial virtues.

Hawks are also considered a symbol of courage and strength. They are often depicted in Japanese literature and art as powerful figures, able to rise above earthly difficulties because of their superior vision and mastery of flight.

The act of young hawks learning to fly offers a rich metaphor for the process by which humans mature and develop.

PERSONAL GROWTH AND DEVELOPMENT

The point at which young hawks learn to fly is a crucial time of transition in an individual's life, reflecting the stage at which young people break away from their dependence on family or community to explore the world. This emancipation represents each person's journey toward autonomy and self-discovery.

CHALLENGING ONE'S LIMITS

Just as hawks must overcome the initial fear of leaving the nest to test their wings, so human beings must also face the uncertainties and fears that accompany significant changes and new ventures. That first flight is a helpful reminder of the need to actively confront fears in order to realize one's potential.

TAKING FLIGHT AGAIN

Learning to fly is not a linear path. It involves falls, defeats, and numerous attempts. This process teaches the art of getting back up after each fall, a fundamental quality for success. Determination and courage are skills that are built by pushing ourselves out of our comfort zone.

FREEDOM AND AUTONOMY

Flight also symbolizes freedom. For young hawks, flying is the ultimate expression of their independence. Similarly, the attainment of psychological maturity for human beings is often marked by the ability to make independent decisions and live in accordance with one's values and aspirations.

Hawks learning to fly reminds us that every new beginning brings with it challenges, but also promises of freedom and opportunities for development. We can find the inspiration to rise above our current circumstances and fly toward our dreams.

LEARNING TO FLY Here the goal is to strengthen your independence and self-esteem through writing and planning. This exercise not only celebrates your journey to greater independence, but also prepares you for flying higher in life's future adventures, just like a young hawk taking flight for the first time.

1 Choose a quiet place where you can reflect without interruption. Bring a journal or tablet with you, so you can record your thoughts and plans.

2 Begin with a personal reflection on the times you have had to learn to fly solo. This could include a new work experience, moving to a new city, or dealing with a difficult situation. Analyze these experiences and describe how you felt.

3 Consider the challenges you faced during these experiences. Reflect on how you reacted, what strategies you used to overcome these difficulties, and what you learned about yourself in the process.

4 Identify and note the personal qualities you developed through these experiences. These might include courage, resilience, adaptability, or self-reliance. Reflect on how these qualities have also influenced other areas of your life.

5 Based on your reflections, set specific goals to continue to develop your independence and self-esteem. Consider new experiences that might push you out of your comfort zone and plan concrete actions to deal with them.

6 Close your eyes and visualize yourself achieving a new goal that requires independence. Imagine successfully navigating the challenges, supported by the qualities you have identified in yourself. Feel the satisfaction and confidence that come from knowing you can face and overcome challenges on your own.

7 Conclude the exercise by acknowledging and appreciating your journey toward independence. Renew your commitment to take the initiative and explore new opportunities to grow. Thank yourself for the courage and determination you have shown so far.

THE GREAT HEAT

大暑

Taisho

WAVES OF HEAT,
CICADAS SING LOUDLY,
AFTERNOON BURNS.

JULY 23–28

THE PAULOWNIA TREE PRODUCES SEEDS

桐始結花 *Kiri hajimete hana o musubu*

Every action you perform today is a seed for the garden of your tomorrow; treat it with wisdom and dedication to cultivate a flourishing future.

Paulownia trees, known in Japan as kiri or empress trees, are prized not only for their impressive growing speed and the beauty of their large leaves and spectacular flowers, but also for their significant symbolic and practical qualities. These trees can reach heights of up to 100 ft (30 m) and are among the fastest growing in the world. Paulownia wood, nicknamed aluminum wood for its lightness and strength, has a variety of uses, from the production of musical instruments and furniture, to shipbuilding and flooring.

In Japan, the tradition is to plant a paulownia tree to mark the birth of a daughter. The tree, once grown, is felled and made into furniture, a valuable gift the girl will receive on her wedding day. This plant is also one of the emblems of the Japanese monarchy, a symbol of good fortune and prosperity, and is often associated with values of femininity and dignity. Its image is so ingrained in Japanese culture that it even appears on 500 yen coins, representing the continuity and harmonious growth of the nation.

FLEXIBILITY AND ADAPTABILITY

Paulownia wood, despite its surprising rapidity of growth, is remarkably strong and light. This intriguing characteristic symbolizes the idea that true strength does not necessarily come from a rigid or heavy structure, and shows us that adaptability and flexibility can be powerful forms of resistance. Often, the ability to adapt to change can reveal itself more effectively than sheer brute strength. This lesson is vital in times of rapid change, suggesting that we may find greater success in flowing with change rather than resisting it.

HOPE AND RENEWAL

Particularly telling is the stage when paulownia trees produce seeds, a moment that evokes the continuity of life and the promise of renewal. The seeds, a symbol of new opportunities and future growth, encourage us to see every conclusion as a possible new beginning. This is a powerful reminder for us to maintain hope and remain open to new possibilities, even when current situations may seem stagnant or blocked. The life cycle of the paulownia reminds us that, although challenges may seem insurmountable, nature itself is geared toward rebirth and renewal.

OVERCOMING OBSTACLES The goal here is to learn how to walk through difficulties. This exercise not only helps you connect with nature and its lessons about resilience and renewal, but also offers a powerful metaphor for reflecting on your personal growth and ability to overcome challenges with grace and determination.

1 Choose a natural trail, preferably in a park or wooded area, where you can walk in peace. Make sure you are wearing comfortable clothing and, if possible, take a notebook or tablet with you to record your reflections.

2 Before you start walking, take a moment to reflect on the goals of the exercise. Set the intention to leave your worries behind and open your mind to the lessons nature can teach you about resilience and renewal.

3 Start walking at a pace you feel comfortable with. As you walk, carefully observe the environment around you. Notice how nature overcomes obstacles: a tree growing around a boulder, plants growing through concrete, and so on. Let these observations inspire thoughts about how you too can overcome challenges in your life.

4 As you walk, enter a meditative state. Focus on your breathing, the rhythm of your steps, and how each step brings you closer to your goal. Reflect on how, despite the obstacles you might encounter, you keep moving forward.

5 Think about the seeds you are planting in your life through your daily actions. What are the seeds you want to plant for your future? How can you nurture them?

6 During or after the walk, take a moment to jot down your reflections in your notebook. Write down what you observed, how you felt, and what seeds you decided to plant in your life.

7 Conclude the exercise by thanking yourself for the time you took to pursue your personal growth and nature for the lessons it taught you. Reacquaint yourself with the beauty and resilience that exists all around you and how you can integrate these qualities into your life.

JULY 29–AUGUST 2

THE EARTH IS DAMP, THE AIR IS HUMID

土潤溽暑 *Tsuchi uruōte mushi atsushi*

When you feel overwhelmed, remember that every difficult moment is an opportunity to demonstrate your strength and hone your ability to resist and give yourself hope.

This time of year is marked by rising temperatures and, for Japanese youth, the end of the school year. It is a time to enjoy refreshing foods such as edamame, juicy tomatoes, and melons, which offer relief from the humidity of summer.

During the period of Taisho, Japan comes alive with lively summer festivals and firework displays. One of the most well-known types of firework is the *senko-hanabi*, traditional Japanese sparklers that light up the evening sky. These delicate fireworks have a strong symbolic charge, as they represent the ephemeral nature of beauty. This ties in with the concept of *mono no aware*, which can be translated as sensitivity to the ephemeral or sadness for transient things, and expresses a feeling of melancholy in the face of the impermanence of beauty.

When we admire something beautiful that we know won't last, like the cherry blossom that blooms beautifully and then falls quickly, we feel a sense of sweet sadness and a deep appreciation for that moment of fleeting beauty. *Mono no aware* teaches us to appreciate life and experiences with a sense of gratitude and awareness of their transient nature. Applying this state of mind to daily life means appreciating fleeting moments, accepting their temporary nature, and drawing strength and awareness from their beauty. This enables us to live with gratitude and to see every experience, whether positive or negative, as an integral part of the cycle of life. One way to practice *mono no aware* in daily life is to take time to appreciate a sunset. Every evening, the sky offers a unique show of colors that rapidly changes from red to purple to the dark blue of night. Knowing that this moment is temporary and unrepeatable can teach us to appreciate it more, to stop and observe it carefully. Even when the sunset ends and gives way to darkness, we can find beauty in the natural cycle of day and night, recognizing that each end brings with it a new beginning. This simple act of contemplation can increase our awareness of—and gratitude for—small daily joys, reinforcing our ability to live in the present.

Another beautiful Japanese tradition at this time of year is the sending of *Shochu-Mimai*: summer greeting cards often featuring images of fireworks, summer flowers, and other seasonal motifs. These cards are a way to inquire about a loved one's health during the height of the heat and update them on personal news. This awareness of impermanence can encourage us to live in the present moment more intensely, to appreciate what we have while we have it, and to let go more easily of what is bound to pass.

MONO NO AWARE This exercise is designed to help you develop a greater consciousness and appreciation for the transient nature of life through direct observation and personal reflection. This exercise allows you to explore the concept of *mono no aware* in a personal and direct way, encouraging a deeper connection with the natural world and your inner experience of life.

1. Find a quiet place outside where you can observe something from nature, such as plants, flowers, or trees. Take a notebook or tablet with you to record your reflections.
2. Begin the exercise by finding a comfortable spot to sit and carefully observe the nature around you. Focus on specific things that catch your attention, such as a flower or the leaves swaying in the breeze.
3. As you watch, think about the ephemeral nature of what you are seeing. Think about how these natural elements change with the seasons, grow, and eventually wither, and how this cycle of life and death is a fundamental part of the existence of every living thing.

4. Reflect on events or aspects of your life that highlight the transitoriness of nature. These may be happy moments that passed quickly or sad experiences that you overcame. Note how these experiences have affected your perception of time and life.
5. Use your notebook or tablet to express your thoughts or feelings. You could write poems, draw pictures, or simply note down thoughts that emerge from the exercise. This is a way to creatively process your reflections and shape your experience of *mono no aware*.
6. Conclude the exercise by expressing gratitude for the ability to experience and appreciate moments of beauty, even if they are fleeting. Commit to bringing this awareness into your daily life, seeking to appreciate and accept the transient nature of everything around you.
7. Reflect on how this exercise has affected your perception of life and its challenges. Think about how you could use this awareness to live a fuller and more meaningful life.

AUGUST 3–7

GREAT RAINS SOMETIMES FALL

大雨時行 *Taiu tokidoki furu*

Even the heaviest rains bring nourishment and new life, reminding us that after every storm a new beginning can arise.

In Japan, this period of heavy downpours sets the stage for the last wave of rainfall before summer ends. This natural phenomenon is crucial for agriculture, as an abundance of water is vital for summer crops such as rice. Rain can be seen as a metaphor for periods of personal turbulence or change. In Japanese thinking there is a deep acceptance of transience and metamorphosis, as exemplified in the concept of *mono no aware*.

This acceptance extends to the way people deal with changes in life, seeing them as opportunities for personal growth and spiritual renewal.

Heavy rains, although they may initially cause discomfort or hardship, eventually enrich the earth. Similarly, difficult periods in our lives, while presenting challenges, can also enrich us, helping us to develop resilience and adaptability.

Appreciating and reflecting on these natural cycles can offer profound lessons about managing changes in life, emphasizing the importance of welcoming each season, whether of nature or in your personal life, with gratitude and openness.

RAIN MEDITATION Cleanse yourself of stress and negativity, and understand that the difficulties you are facing will pass.

1. Find a quiet place where you can sit without being disturbed. If possible, a place where you can hear or imagine the sound of rain.
2. Begin with deep breaths. With each inhalation, feel fresh air coming in, and with each exhalation, release any tension. Close your eyes.
3. Imagine you are in a garden full of greenery. You can feel the moist, fresh air on your face. The garden is nourished by gentle rain. Listen to the soothing sound of water falling on lush leaves and filling the air with a promise of renewal.
4. Think about releasing negativity or stress with each exhalation. Reconnect with the earth and with each inhalation, feel the renewing power of the rain cleansing you.
5. Reflect on the temporary nature of the great rains and how even difficult times in your life are temporary.
6. Give thanks for the resources that support you during stormy times. Feel gratitude for the storms. Slowly begin to bring your attention to the present. Open your eyes, taking this serenity and the lessons learned with you.

HINTS OF AUTUMN

立秋

Risshū

EVENING COOLNESS,
SWEET BREATH OF
AUTUMN,
LEAVES DIE.

AUGUST 8–12

COOL WINDS BLOW

涼風至 *Suzukaze itaru*

Every change brings with it a breath of freshness, opens new doors, and offers new mountains to climb and vistas to explore.

In the heart of the Japanese summer, the *Suzukaze itaru* microseason marks the arrival of cool winds, a climatic shift that brings relief from the summer heat. These winds not only moderate the high temperatures but also bring a symbolic change, indicating the gradual transition into autumn. This period is especially valued for its power to refresh both the environment and people's spirits, offering a restorative break from the intense summer days.

The winds symbolize the ability to sweep away the old and welcome the new, inviting us to reflect on how we can apply this principle of renewal to our daily lives.

GET RID OF WHAT WE DON'T NEED

The cooling of the air can inspire us to rid ourselves of habits, thoughts, and relationships that no longer serve our well-being. Just as cool winds cleanse the atmosphere, so we can use this period to perform a kind of mental clearing, removing psychological clutter that might hinder our personal growth.

MENTAL AND PHYSICAL RENEWAL

Relief from the heat can also be seen as a symbol of mental and physical renewal. This is an ideal time to adopt new healthy habits, both mentally and physically. Whether it's starting a new exercise routine, meditating more regularly, or simply devoting more time to reflection and rest, cool winds remind us of the importance of taking care of ourselves.

WELCOMING CHANGE

In addition, the arrival of cool winds teaches us the importance of co-mingling change with openness and optimism. Change can be difficult, but it is also an inevitable part of life. Accepting and embracing change can transform situations that intimidate us into exciting opportunities for development and self-improvement.

Ultimately, this microseason offers us a precious opportunity to reflect and act. It is a time to assess what we have accumulated—physically, emotionally, and mentally—and decide what we want to carry forward and what to leave behind. This period can serve as a reminder to renew our commitment to personal growth and transformation, allowing us to move into the cooler months with renewed clarity and lightness.

LETTING GO OF WHAT WE NO LONGER NEED This exercise is designed to help you identify and dispense with the superfluous elements in your life, whether these are physical objects, habits, or thoughts, allowing you to make room for the new and the beneficial. This exercise will also help you develop a greater awareness and appreciation for what adds true value to your existence.

1. Find a quiet place where you can sit comfortably without distraction. Bring a notebook or tablet with you to jot down your reflections and decisions.
2. Begin by taking a few minutes to reflect on what in your

life is superfluous. It could be material objects, relationships that are no longer meaningful, harmful habits, or old ways of thinking.

3 Make an inventory of the areas of your life that could benefit from a cleanse. This could include your physical space (home or office), your daily routine, your diet, your hobbies, or your social interactions. Note down specific items or aspects that you feel are superfluous or do not add value to your life.

4 For each item or aspect listed, ask yourself, "Do I still need it? Does it contribute to my happiness or well-being? Could I live without it?" Be honest in your answers and reflect on how each item affects your life.

5 Decide which of the elements you are ready to let go of. This may signify throwing away physical objects, discontinuing unhealthy habits, distancing yourself from toxic relationships, or abandoning old patterns of thinking. Make a plan for how and when you will achieve this.

6 Put your plan into action. It might mean scheduling days to clean your house, change your routine, consult a health professional, or take steps to improve relationships. Action can take time, so set realistic deadlines for yourself.

7 After completing these actions, reflect on how you feel. What has been the impact of letting go of unnecessary aspects of your life? Do you feel lighter, happier, or more energized? Consider how this process of letting go has changed your perception of what is truly important.

8 Conclude the exercise by expressing gratitude for the courage it has taken to make space in your life. Commit to keeping this space clean and open to new experiences and opportunities. Reflect on how you can apply this exercise of letting go periodically to continue to grow and renew yourself.

AUGUST 13–17

EVENINGS ARE FULL OF THE SONG OF CICADAS

寒蝉鳴 *Higurashi naku*

Like the cicadas that sing fearlessly as the sun goes down, we too can find the courage to sing our own unique song, celebrating each transitional moment in life.

The evening cicada song, known in Japan as *Higurashi naku*, marks the transition from daylight to the tranquility of night. This offers a time to reconnect with oneself following the hustle and bustle of the day.

The song of the cicadas also signals the impending change of season from warm to more temperate, reminding us of the constant evolution of life and the transience of each phase.

Often, during the busyness of daily life, we suppress our deepest thoughts or avoid dealing with complex emotions. The song of the cicadas, with its piercing and meditative call, can serve as a reminder to listen to our inner voice, thus offering a space and time for feelings or thoughts that have been ignored or minimized during the day. Through this symbolic end of the summer, we can find peace in change and transition, and perhaps discover new perspectives and new strengths within ourselves.

SUNSET This exercise encourages introspection and meditation through the daily transitional moment of sunset. Bring a notebook or tablet with you to jot down your reflections.

1. Find a quiet place where you can see the sky at sunset. Sit comfortably and begin with a few deep breaths to center yourself.
2. Open your eyes and observe the sky. Notice the changes in color and light.

3. Think about the different phases of the day and what impact they had. Note the most productive times of the day.
4. As the sun sets, bring your attention to your inner state. What feelings emerge? Relief, sadness, peace? Note them down.
5. Think of an area of your life that is going through a transition. Reflect on how you are managing this transition.
6. As the sun goes down, consider what you would like to bring into the new day. Write down your hopes or goals for tomorrow.

AUGUST 18–22

DENSE MISTS HIDE THE WORLD

蒙霧升降 *Fukaki kiri matō*

Even in the thickest fog, each step forward illuminates the path ahead, reminding us that clarity can emerge from uncertainty.

During *Fukaki kiri matō*, it is common for dense layers of fog to form and descend over the landscape, a phenomenon particularly visible in mountainous areas and near waterways. This fog not only visually transforms the environment, shrouding everything in a veil of mystery and stillness, it also marks a transitional phase in Japan's seasonal climate as the country prepares to bid farewell to summer and welcome autumn.

The presence of fog at this time of year is influenced by temperature variations between day and night, which increase the level of condensation in the air. This natural phenomenon evokes feelings of introspection and reflection. Dense fog invites one to slow down and reflect, offering a moment of contemplative pause before autumn's renewal. It can alter our perception of the landscape, masking familiar contours, and creating an ambience of mystery and indefinability. Similarly, during periods of uncertainty in our lives, the clear contours of our expectations and plans can become blurred and indeterminate, forcing us to navigate without a clear map.

WHAT CAN FOG TEACH US?

The properties of the fog can teach us many lessons, thereby providing tools for managing our lives.

Slow down: Fog imposes a slowdown. In life, this can result in more thoughtful decisions, as we have time to assess complex situations without rushing.

Sharpen the senses: With reduced visibility, other senses are enhanced. In moments of uncertainty, we can develop greater attentiveness to internal insights and perceptions that might be overlooked when everything seems clear.

Accepting the unknown: The fog teaches us that we do not always see the complete path ahead. Instead of struggling with uncertainty, we learn to embrace it as an inevitable part of life's journey. This acceptance can reduce anxiety and fear of the unknown.

Adaptation: Just as a navigator must quickly adapt to changing conditions when the fog descends, so we can develop greater flexibility. Adaptability does not mean lack of preparedness, but rather the ability to change plans and strategies in response to new information or circumstances.

Seeking support: Navigating through a thick fog often requires the help of tools or support from others. This can be compared to seeking counseling, emotional support, or guidance from mentors.

The microseason of dense fog invites us to consider how uncertainty can be transformed from a state to be feared into a condition from which we can learn and grow.

NAVIGATING THE FOG This exercise is designed to help you develop strategies for confronting periods of uncertainty, inspired by the dense fog that sometimes covers our visual and mental landscapes. It not only helps you develop resilience, but also promotes a greater awareness of how we can find our way, even when the path is unclear.

1 Find a quiet place where you can sit comfortably without distraction. Bring a notebook or tablet with you to jot down your reflections.

2 Start with a few deep breaths to center yourself. Close your eyes and imagine that you are in a landscape shrouded in fog. Visualize a thick fog that limits your view to a few steps ahead and feel the moisture in the air.

3 Reflect on an area of your current life that you feel is shrouded in the haze of uncertainty. It could be an important decision you need to make, a professional or personal situation that is unclear, or any other aspect of your life that you feel is uncertain.

4 Note down strategies that you might use to navigate through this fog. Consider approaches such as asking for advice, taking small steps to test different directions, increasing your awareness and intuition, or even using supportive tools such as planning and analysis.

5 Choose a strategy to try in the current situation. Plan how you will implement this strategy in the coming days and what resources or support you may need.

6 After trying the strategy, reflect on its effectiveness in providing you with direction through the fog. Consider what worked, what didn't, and how you might modify your approach in the future.

7 Conclude the exercise by reflecting on how this process has helped you see more clearly through the fog and what lessons you can take with you to deal with future uncertainty.

THE HEAT LOOSENS ITS GRIP

処暑

Shosho

HEAT FADES.
LEAVES SIGH.
EVENING BREEZE.

AUGUST 23–27

THE COTTON FLOWERS BLOOM

綿柎開 *Wata no hana shibe hiraku*

Even the slowest progress is progress; every step, no matter how small, brings us closer to the realization of our dreams.

The microseason of cotton flowers provides an example of how beauty and significance can reside in the less conspicuous things in the natural world. Similarly, in our personal and professional lives, it is often the less obvious tasks or steady progress that provide the foundations for future successes. This period invites us to respect the imperceptible process of growth that occurs beneath the surface, preparing us for future accomplishments. This awareness can increase our appreciation for those small daily actions that are helpful in achieving long-term goals. In a culture that often values quick results and big wins, the growth of the cotton flower, which takes time and is not immediately visible, reminds us that patience is an essential element in staying motivated, even when progress is imperceptible. Just as cotton flowers cannot be forced to bloom before they are ready, so our goals and projects also have a natural rhythm that must be respected. Learning to accept and work with this natural rhythm, rather than against it, can reduce stress and increase our effectiveness.

CULTIVATE PATIENCE In this exercise you will reflect on a time when your patience has been tested and use your reflections to create strategies to better manage situations in the future.

1. Find a place where you can sit without distraction. Take a notebook or tablet with you to jot down your reflections.
2. Sit down, close your eyes, and focus on your breath. Begin with a few deep breaths: count to four as you inhale, hold your breath

for three to four seconds, then exhale counting to eight. Repeat this breathing cycle for several minutes.

3 Think of a situation in which you have lost your patience. Try to visualize the scene, including the people involved, the environment, and what was said or done that triggered your impatience.

4 Reflect on the emotions you felt at that moment. Write down your observations. Try to understand the reason for these emotions. Perhaps there were unmet expectations, or you were under pressure.

5 Now that you have identified your emotions, reflect on how you reacted. Did it make the situation better or worse? Write down some alternatives for handling the situation more patiently.

6 Develop strategies that you can use in the future when you find yourself in similar situations such as breathing techniques, a mantra to remind you to remain calm, or taking a short break.

7 Commit to practicing the strategies you have developed. You can start with small steps, such as being more patient with yourself when you make mistakes, or trying to better understand others' points of view before formulating a response.

AUGUST 28–SEPTEMBER 1

SUMMER HEAT FADES AWAY

天地始粛 *Tenchi hajimete samushi*

As the heat of summer gives way to the coolness of autumn, let us remember that each season of life offers its own unique gift of transformation and renewal.

The transition from the heat of summer to the milder temperatures of autumn represents a profound spiritual transition. During the summer, energy is high, days are long, we often engage in hectic activities, and opportunities for socializing are greater. However, as summer fades and the days begin to shorten gradually, nature itself invites us to slow down, signaling that it is time to enter a more reflective and composed phase.

This microseason encourages us to reflect on the cyclical nature of life and our reactions to constant change. It is an invitation to let go of excess energy and stress, allowing the first breezes of autumn to bring freshness and new perspectives. Embracing the change of seasons with a balanced attitude means embracing both release and acceptance: letting go of what no longer serves us and welcoming new opportunities and challenges. The cooling weather can be seen as a metaphorical sigh of relief, a time to reconsider your goals and align your own actions with your greatest aspirations. It is also an ideal time to review life and work strategies.

As the landscape around us begins to show signs of change, we can explore our inner mind. It is time to ask ourselves, "In what ways am I growing? What am I learning from these experiences? How can I better prepare myself for the coming months?"

Ultimately, *Tenchi hajimete samushi* represents not only a change in temperature, but it is also a signal of renewal. By embracing the change with a balanced attitude, we can use this transition to improve our lives.

EMBRACING CHANGE As the weather cools, take this opportunity to sit comfortably and take stock of where you are in your life, how you have managed change, and how you would like to renew yourself.

1. Find a quiet place to sit without distractions. Bring a notebook or tablet with you to jot down your reflections. Start with a few deep breaths to center yourself. Close your eyes. Feel the cooler air begin to replace the stifling heat of summer.
2. Think about the last few months of your life. What have been the hot periods, both literally and metaphorically? What challenges have you faced that are now beginning to subside? Reflect on

how the arrival of the cool autumn weather may symbolize new opportunities or a welcome change in your life. Is there something you are particularly grateful for that is ending or changing? What new opportunities or experiences might be propitiated by this change?

3 Consider how you can use this period of transition to renew yourself.

4 Conclude the exercise by expressing gratitude for the changes you are experiencing. Note down a specific commitment you want to make to welcome this new climate into your life.

SEPTEMBER 2–7

THE RICE RIPENS

禾乃登 *Kokumono sunawachi minoru*

Perseverance turns even the smallest seed into an abundant harvest; never underestimate the power of time and tenacity.

Rice is an integral part of the Japanese diet as well as the country's culture, religion, and social practices. Since ancient times, rice has been more than just a food: it has been considered sacred, a gift from the gods, and a symbol of prosperity and well-being. In Japan, rice cultivation dates back more than 2,000 years. Rice was so valuable that it was used as currency and as an offering at temples in Shinto ceremonies. It is also the focus of many festivals, such as the *Niinamesai*, a festival in which the Emperor of Japan offers freshly harvested rice as a tribute to the gods.

Rice cultivation in Japan follows an annual cycle that begins with planting in the spring and culminates in the autumn harvest. This cycle of growth and renewal can be seen as a metaphor for human life. Growing rice requires considerable patience and attention. Each season brings a range of challenges, such as floods or droughts, which growers must face with resilience and adaptability. This patience can inspire us to keep calm and persevere. Rice cultivation emphasizes the importance of community and mutual support both in rice cultivation and in other human activities. A successful harvest depends on harmony and teamwork.

Ultimately, in Japan rice is much more than a staple food—it is a powerful symbol of life, community, and interdependence. Through the cycle of its growth and the traditions that surround it, rice continues to teach lessons in patience, resilience, and collaboration.

CELEBRATE THE HARVEST Apply the metaphor of the harvest and the work involved to your own life, reflecting on past successes and how these can help shape future endeavors.

1. Find a place where you can sit without distraction. Bring a notebook or tablet to jot down your reflections. Start with a few deep breaths to center yourself. Close your eyes and focus your attention on your breathing.
2. Think about the projects or goals you have cultivated over the past months or years. Reflect on the results of these efforts. What were the successes? What did you learn in the process? Were there particularly rewarding or revealing moments? Consider how each step contributed to the end result.
3. Consider what lessons you have learned from the growth and development of your projects. How have these experiences influenced your vision of perseverance and hard work? Have there been changes in the way you approach new challenges?
4. Based on your successes and the lessons learned, think about how you might apply this knowledge to future projects or goals. What new seeds do you want to plant? What strategies have helped you get the best results?
5. Conclude the exercise by expressing gratitude for the harvest you have obtained and the opportunities for growth you have had. Commit to carrying forward the wisdom within this reflection.

THE SHINING DEW

白露

Hakuro

FRESH AWAKENING.
MORNING STARS SHINE.
SILENT GRASS.

SEPTEMBER 8–12

DEW GLISTENS ON THE GRASS

草露白 *Kusa no tsuyu shiroshi*

Each morning offers us a blank canvas; the dew on the grass reminds us to appreciate the pure and simple beauty that every new day brings.

The microseason *Kusa no tsuyu shiroshi* evokes a vision of pureness and delicacy: watching the dew reflecting the first rays of the sun can be a moment of silent meditation and deep connection with nature.

As morning dew is so ephemeral, in literature and poetry it often symbolizes the impermanence of life and the fleeting beauty of moments. In Japan, this is intimately related to the concept of *mono no aware* (see page 94), the sensitivity to the fleeting nature of things and the sweet melancholy that arises from this knowledge. This phenomenon is a natural invitation to the practice of present-moment awareness, because it requires a careful and concentrated gaze to be truly appreciated. The act of observing the dew can become a form of meditation, which can help center the thoughts and calm the mind.

The microseason *Kusa no tsuyu shiroshi* is a reminder of the beauty in impermanence and the possibility of daily renewal. Through reflection, we can find peace in the ephemeral and strength in the freshness of each new day, learning to live with greater awareness and gratitude.

APPRECIATING THE BEAUTY AROUND US Use this daily meditation on the morning dew to recognize, appreciate, and accept the impermanence of beauty.

1. Choose a quiet place to be outside, ideally where you can see grass and dew in the morning, or another symbol of renewal. Take a journal or tablet with you.
2. Spend a few moments in silence. Breathe deeply and observe the dew on the grass. Notice how the drops reflect light and how each detail is enhanced by the moisture.
3. Reflect on how dew, while ephemeral, adds beauty and vitality to the grass each morning. Consider how this phenomenon can parallel aspects of your life that are temporary but precious.
4. In your journal or on your tablet write down at least three everyday things you notice and are grateful for. This could include moments of natural beauty, positive interactions with others, or any small successes.
5. Take a moment to recognize that each day is a new beginning which offers opportunities for growth and change.
6. At the end of the week, reflect on how this exercise has affected your perception of daily beauty and impermanence.

SEPTEMBER 13–17

THE SONG OF THE WAGTAILS

鶺鴒鳴 *Sekirei naku*

In the stillness of dawn, find your inner strength; every moment of silence is an invitation to be reborn.

The microseason of *Sekirei naku* celebrates the time when birds from the wagtail family (Motacillidae) fill the air with their songs. This event marks a transitional phase and heralds the arrival of autumn with a symphony of sounds that awakens awareness and sensitivity. Wagtails, known as ballerinas in Japan, are named for their graceful movements and lively behavior, and play an important role during this change of season, representing a powerful metaphor for human communication. Just as these birds use song to connect and make their presence known, we too use our voice to express ideas, emotions, and make connections. Their ability to sing reminds us of the importance of clarity and beauty in the art of communication.

The song of these birds urges us to explore and value our personal expression. In a hectic world often overwhelmed by noise, finding the courage and space to authentically express ourselves is vital to our psychological well-being. These birds teach us that every voice has the power to be heard and to make a difference. Their song encourages us to find our own unique voice and to use it not only to affirm our identity, but also to enrich and positively influence the community around us. It challenges us to reflect on our capacity for expression, emphasizing the intrinsic value of each individual contribution to the great chorus of life.

FIND YOUR VOICE Use this exercise to compare how you usually express yourself with your unfiltered, authentic self and see what you can learn about your voice.

1. Choose a place where you feel comfortable, without distractions. Bring a notebook or tablet with you to record your thoughts. Sit down and reflect on how you usually express yourself. Think about situations in which you felt your voice was heard and those in which you felt it was not. Note down these reflections.
2. Set a timer for 5 minutes and start writing or talking about a topic that is particularly close to your heart. Don't worry about form; focus on the free flow of thought. The goal is to express yourself unfiltered.

3. Re-read what you have written or listen again to what you have recorded. Pay attention to your tone, the words you chose, and the way you structured your thoughts. Ask yourself, "Do my words truly reflect what I feel? Is there consistency between what I say and what I feel?"
4. Reflect on the differences between how you normally express yourself and how you freely expressed yourself in this exercise. Think about what you would retain as part of your daily expression and what you could change to be more authentic.
5. Set a goal to practice authentic expression. At the end of the week, take a few minutes to evaluate how these practices have affected your ability to express yourself. Reflect on how you felt and what you learned about yourself and your voice.

SEPTEMBER 18–22

THE MIGRATION OF THE SWALLOWS

玄鳥去 *Tsubame saru*

As the swallows fly south, let us remember that every departure is also an invitation to interpret our dreams and explore new paths.

The *Tsubame saru* microseason offers an opportunity to observe the natural cycle of swallows as they embark on their migrations to warmer climates. That spectacular annual journey is necessary for survival, but it is also a powerful symbol of the inevitable transitions we all face in life.

When embarking on their migration, swallows leave the safety of their roosts, driven by survival instinct and the search for better living conditions. Similarly, in human life, we are often called to step out of our comfort zone in order to increase and realize our potential. Their journey reminds us that change, despite the fears it creates and its uncertainties, is full of possibilities and is necessary for our development.

The migration of the swallow prompts us to let go of what no longer serves us. This can include relationships, habits, outdated beliefs, and even old ways of thinking that could hold back our progress. Letting go gives us the opportunity to move freely toward new experiences. Despite the dangers and uncertainties, swallows undertake their flight tirelessly, accepting an invitation to face life's challenges with similar courage, always maintaining hope.

Tsubame saru can inspire us to evaluate situations in our life, to consider what we need to leave behind, and to embrace the changes necessary for our growth. Like the swallows, we can learn to see each goodbye not just as an end, but also as the prelude to new beginnings and adventures.

LEAVING THE NEST This exercise will help you identify and push through the barriers of your comfort zone, encouraging you to take steps toward new experiences that can enrich your life.

1. Choose a place where you can reflect without interruption. Make sure to have a notebook or a tablet to jot down your thoughts and discoveries.
2. Begin by listing the activities, situations, and environments in which you feel most comfortable. These can range from daily routines to social interactions in family groups or specific work environments. Reflect on what holds you back from exploring beyond these comfort zones. What makes you afraid of the unknown? What beliefs do you hold about change? Write down at least three thoughts or beliefs that limit you.
3. Set small goals that push you beyond your comfort zones. After putting these into practice, reflect on the experience: how did it feel? What aspects were less intimidating than you thought? Was there anything positively surprising?
4. As you become more comfortable with these small steps, gradually continue to expand your goals.

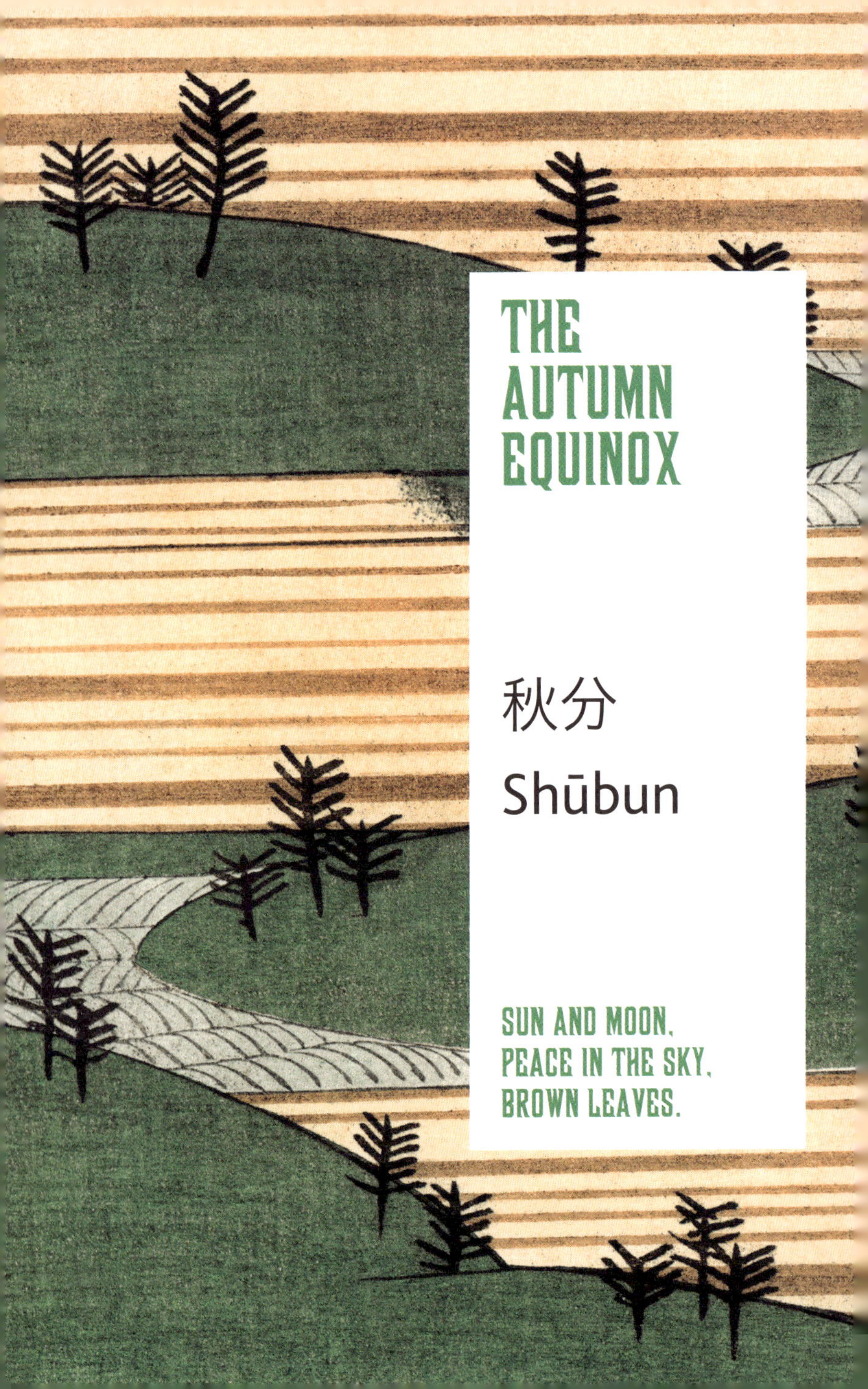

THE AUTUMN EQUINOX

秋分

Shūbun

SUN AND MOON,
PEACE IN THE SKY,
BROWN LEAVES.

SEPTEMBER 23–27

THE THUNDER CEASES

雷乃収声 *Kaminari sunawachi koe o osamu*

When the roar of thunder subsides, the silence that follows invites us to reflect and find peace in the stillness that remains.

The previous appearance of thunder in the Japanese calendar (*Kaminari sunawachi koe o hassu*, page 38) is seen as a prelude to the storms and rains that refresh the earth and stimulate growth. In contrast, the ending of the storms during this microseason brings with it a sense of resolution and calm, a sign that the summer rains are over and the serenity of autumn has begun. This time of year provides an opportunity for deep reflection on the transitions each of us faces. The last of the thunder, marking the end of the tumultuous activity of summer and the beginning of the quiet of autumn, invites us to meditate on the cyclical nature of change and its inevitability in life. The transition from a period of frequent, loud activity to one of quiet represents not only a seasonal change, but is also a powerful metaphor for personal periods of transformation. After the clamor and frenzy, the silence that follows thunder allows us to assimilate lived experiences and recover inner equilibrium. This transition can be compared to moments in life where, after intense challenges or major changes, there is an opportunity for reflection, regeneration, and renewal. Just as nature slowly recovers from the dynamism of summer, we too can find moments of calm to process and reframe our experiences. This period symbolizes an opportunity to leave behind old fears or worries and embrace a new beginning with a renewed and more serene perspective.

Psychologically, the peace that follows the roar can be very beneficial. It teaches us the importance of finding moments of stillness in our hectic lives. This stillness is not only found in our surroundings, but is also internal, allowing us to access a space of deep inner peace.

In a world that values productivity exclusively, recognizing the importance of rest and reflection can be transformative.

Each phase of stillness after tumult can serve as a powerful reminder of our resilience and adaptability. Learning to navigate through changes, adapt, and find serenity in silence can strengthen our ability to cope with future uncertainties. This process of continuous adaptation and growth is critical to our personal development and mental well-being.

THE CALM AFTER THE STORM This exercise is designed to help you restore calm after experiencing moments of intense emotion or stress. The goal is to develop strategies to better manage emotional reactions and regain inner balance, thereby reducing the impact of stress and promoting greater emotional resilience. With regular practice, you can more easily find your inner calm and face life's challenges with greater serenity.

1. Find a quiet place where you can sit or lie down comfortably without being disturbed.
2. Begin by breathing deeply to calm the nervous system. Inhale slowly counting to four, hold your breath for a count of four, then exhale slowly for a count of eight. Repeat this breathing cycle for a few minutes until you feel more relaxed.
3. Recall an episode in which you felt overwhelmed by your emotions or lost control. Recognize the emotion or feeling you experienced. Name the emotion, whether it is fear, anxiety, anger, or sadness. Admitting what you are feeling is the first step to being able to manage that emotion.
4. Accept the emotion without judgment. Acknowledge that it is normal to experience a wide range of feelings and that every emotion is valid. Say to yourself something like, "It is normal to feel this way. It is human to have these reactions."

5. Close your eyes and imagine a place that represents peace and release. It could be a beach, a forest, your special room, or an imaginary place. Visualize yourself in this place, feeling every detail that contributes to calm, such as sounds, lights, and sensations.
6. While maintaining the image of your safe place, talk to yourself using reassuring and motivating phrases. Use positive affirmations such as "I have the strength to get through this moment" or "Every moment of tension is also an opportunity to grow and learn."
7. When you feel ready, slowly bring your attention back to the present. Gently move your fingers and toes, and when you feel completely present and calm, open your eyes.
8. Take a moment to reflect on the experience. Write down what you learned and how you might use this exercise in future situations of intense stress or emotion.

SEPTEMBER 28–OCTOBER 2

INSECTS RETREAT UNDERGROUND

蟄虫坏戸 *Mushi kakurete to o fusagu*

Taking time for rest is not a luxury, but a vital necessity that prepares the ground for future growth and innovation.

At this time of year, insects seek shelter underground to prepare for the cold season, demonstrating an extraordinary ability to adapt to adverse environmental conditions. This survival strategy highlights the importance of adequately preparing for periods of potential difficulty. Similarly, each of us can learn from the behavior of these tiny creatures by recognizing the value of preparation and rest before facing our own cold seasons, which may manifest in the form of work stress, personal challenges, or life changes.

THE VALUE OF REST

The value of rest is a concept that deserves to be considered in depth, especially in a cultural context that often glorifies incessant activity and productivity. In this context, taking time to rest may seem not only counterintuitive, but sometimes even impractical. However, rest is not just a break from action—it is a vital ingredient for a healthy and productive existence.

During sleep and periods of relaxation, the body performs essential functions of cell repair and renewal, hormone regulation, and memory consolidation. Without adequate rest, the body does not function at its maximum potential, leading to decreased performance, increased vulnerability to disease, and a general decline in health.

In parallel, rest has a significant impact on mental health. Taking time to relax and disconnect helps you to de-stress, manage anxiety, and combat depression. These periods of calm allow the mind to unwind, reflect, and reorganize, improving its ability to make decisions, solve problems, and generate creative ideas.

Resilience is influenced by the quality and quantity of the rest we allow ourselves. Mindful rest helps build greater mental flexibility, providing people with the strength to face challenges and adapt to adversity. Without adequate moments of rest, individuals can become exhausted, which increases stress and the risk of burnout.

Periods of rest provide a unique opportunity for reflection, which is essential for personal growth and development. These moments allow people to reflect on their progress, evaluate future directions, and realign actions with personal values and goals. Rest can thus serve as a time for deep introspection, where mindful decisions can be made that will positively influence one's life path.

Recognizing the value of rest involves more than admitting its necessity: it requires actively integrating restful practices into your everyday routines. This may include establishing an evening routine that promotes restful sleep, planning breaks during work, and participating in relaxing activities.

INTEGRATING REST INTO YOUR DAILY LIFE This exercise is designed to help you integrate moments of rest into your daily routine, improving your overall well-being and productivity. Through simple but effective steps, you will learn how to make rest a regular part of your lifestyle. Integrating rest not only improves your physical and mental well-being but can also lead to greater efficiency and satisfaction in your daily activities. Through the regular implementation of break times, you can build a more balanced and sustainable life.

1. Find a quiet place where you can reflect without distraction. Make sure to have a notebook or tablet to jot down your plans and reflections.
2. Begin by writing down your current daily routine, including both work and leisure time. Identify times when you feel most stressed or fatigued.
3. As you look at your routine, identify times when you might be able to introduce short periods of rest. These can be 5–10-minute intervals between commitments or longer periods, once or twice a week.
4. Decide what types of rest activities you would like to incorporate, such as a quick walk, reading a book, or doing a short meditation.
5. Begin by integrating these moments of rest into your day. It is important to treat these rest times with the same seriousness as the other appointments in your calendar.
6. At the end of the week, reflect on the effectiveness of this new practice. Consider which moments of rest have been most effective and which might need modification. Decide how to make them a permanent part of your life.

OCTOBER 3–7

FARMERS PREPARE THE FIELDS

水始涸 *Mizu hajimete karuru*

Preparing for change is akin to making the fields ready for plowing: it requires commitment and perseverance, but the fruits of this labor will lead to the reaping of new fruits and an abundance of future possibilities.

In Japanese culture, tending the earth is often seen as a meditative practice, where respect for—and understanding of—natural rhythms is essential. In this context, plowing symbolizes a renewal, not only of the earth but also of the soul. Just as the earth is turned over to expose fresh, fertile layers, so we can take advantage of moments of transition in our lives to turn our attention inward, uncovering the parts of us left unexplored or neglected.

The fields of our mind—our heart and spirit—can accumulate weeds in the form of poor habits, prejudices, and beliefs that hinder our growth and well-being. Just as the farmer meticulously removes debris and weeds, so we can engage in inner cleansing, removing thoughts and behaviors that no longer serve us.

This cleansing and preparation process requires care and a respect for the natural timing of our personal evolution. Plowing is not a brutal act, but rather a way of making space, aerating the soil, and allowing new connections to emerge.

PLOWING YOUR INNER FIELD This exercise helps you reflect on how you can plow the field of your inner life by removing unnecessary or harmful habits, beliefs, and behaviors, and prepare the ground for personal growth and development.

1. Start with a short meditation to center yourself. Close your eyes, breathe deeply, and focus your attention on your breath. Allow each exhalation to relax you more deeply.
2. Identify the weeds. Think about the areas in your life that should be cleaned up. These can be relationships, work commitments, habits, or thought patterns.
3. Think about how you could plow these areas to remove obstacles and prepare yourself for new beginnings. What habits can you break? What aspects of your life or people need to be given less time or energy on your part?
4. Develop a concrete plan for each area you have identified. This could include setting limits, ending harmful behaviors, seeking professional support, or devoting time to personal development.
5. Evaluate progress periodically. Be flexible and willing to make adjustments to your plan. Renewal is an ongoing process, not a single event.

WINTER IS COMING; THE DEW IS COLD

寒露

Kanro

THE DEW COOLS,
KEEPS THE SECRETS
OF THE NIGHT.
MOON OVERSEES.

OCTOBER 8–12

THE WILD GEESE RETURN

鴻雁来 *Kōgan kitaru*

Sail through the winds of change with the determination and grace of one who knows that after every voyage a new dawn awaits us, ready to light our path to the future.

The wild geese return to Japan from their summer breeding grounds in Siberia at this time, then return north with the arrival of spring. This seasonal migration, governed by natural rhythms, represents a cycle of departures and returns. These birds face countless challenges during their journey, including adverse weather conditions, predators, and long flights. Their ability to overcome these difficulties and return each year teaches us that despite adversity, we can find the strength to persevere and return to our fundamental landmarks. These elements in our lives give us stability, direction, and a sense of belonging. They include:

Personal values: Principles such as integrity, kindness, perseverance, and gratitude guide our behavior and decisions. Returning to our core values helps us to remain consistent in times of uncertainty.

Meaningful relationships: Connections with family, friends, and community are essential to our emotional well-being. These relationships provide us with support and a sense of belonging, especially during difficult times.

Places: Physical places, such as one's home or a sacred place, can have special meaning for us and returning to them can offer a sense of peace and connection to the past. They remind us of who we are and where we came from, offering a broader perspective during times of change.

Rituals: Daily or weekly practices, such as meditation or exercise, help us stay centered and provide structure, especially during times of transition.

Aspirations: Clear goals provide us with direction and purpose in life. They help us stay focused and motivated, even when we encounter obstacles. They are our North Star in times of doubt and uncertainty.

When life becomes chaotic or when we face significant challenges, it is easy to feel lost or disoriented. It is at these times that returning to our fundamental points of reference becomes crucial. These reference points act as guides, reminding us of who we are and what is truly important to us.

PLOTTING THE COURSE This exercise is designed to help you identify and reflect on your core reference points—those principles, relationships, places, practices, and goals that provide you with stability, direction, and a sense of belonging. Make a habit of regularly reflecting on your foundational reference points. This will help you stay connected to what is truly important to you and navigate through challenges with greater resilience and clarity.

1. Find a place where you can sit comfortably without being disturbed. Bring a notebook or tablet to jot down your reflections.
2. Write down the values you consider most important in your life. How do they influence your daily choices and relationships?
3. Reflect on the people who have a significant impact in your life. Write down the family members, friends, colleagues, or people in your community who you consider crucial to your emotional well-being and reflect on how these relationships support you.
4. Write a list of the places that give you a sense of peace and connection. Reflect on what makes them meaningful.
5. Reflect on habits and rituals that help you stay centered and connected with yourself. These may include meditation, exercise, reading, or any other practice that helps you maintain balance.

6 Write a list of your short- and long-term goals and reflect on how these give you direction and purpose in life.

7 After you have completed your reflections on each of the areas listed opposite, review your notes and see if any themes or common connections emerge. These represent your core reference points. Recognizing and nurturing these can help you find stability and direction, especially during times of change or difficulty.

OCTOBER 13–17

THE CHRYSANTHEMUMS ARE IN BLOOM

菊花開 *Kiku no hana hiraku*

Just like chrysanthemums that thrive in the cool of autumn, we too can embrace change and flourish in new circumstances.

In Japan, the chrysanthemum, known as *kiku*, is a symbol of great importance, closely associated with the imperial family. According to ancient traditions, members of Japan's imperial dynasty are directly descended from the sun goddess, Amaterasu. This divine lineage helps explain the association between the empire and the golden chrysanthemum, both of which serve as solar symbols. The Japanese emperor, considered the manifestation of the divine will on Earth, acts as a bridge between the divine and the mortal, reflecting the purity of the chrysanthemum.

Chrysanthemums bloom in autumn, a season of transition, and are thus a symbol of resilience and inner strength. Their ability to thrive at a time when many other plants begin to decay symbolizes tenacity and the ability to find beauty even in the most difficult conditions.

Like the chrysanthemums that bloom in the autumn cold, we too can cope with the challenges of life with courage and determination. Even when circumstances seem unfavorable, we can find ways to adapt and thrive. Not only that—these flowers remind us that difficulties can be turned into opportunities for growth. Even when everything around us seems to fade, we can find within ourselves the strength to be reborn and shine. Most importantly, chrysanthemums teach us to see beauty in stages of transition and change.

FINDING BEAUTY IN CHANGE This exercise will help you recognize and appreciate beauty during stages of change in your life, inspired by the blooming of chrysanthemums.

1. Think about recent changes in your life. Record these changes in your notebook or tablet.
2. Reflect on how these changes have brought new opportunities or revealed hidden beauty. Jot down at least three positive aspects of your life that came out of these changes.
3. Write a statement of acceptance for each change identified, expressing gratitude for the opportunities it has brought.
4. Note any practical steps to maintain this mindset in the future.

OCTOBER 18–22

CRICKETS CHIRP AROUND THE DOORWAY

蟋蟀在戸 *Kirigirisu to ni ari*

The song of crickets is an invitation to slow down, to enjoy the beauty of nature, and to find peace in the simple joys of life.

In Japanese culture, crickets are valued for their melodious song, which heralds the arrival of autumn and invites reflection and contemplation. In the past, the Japanese liked to keep crickets in cages to listen to them sing, finding in them a source of inner peace. The constant trilling of these insects offers us a natural invitation to stop and take time for ourselves.

In a hectic world, contemplation becomes a valuable practice. When we take the time to reflect on our experiences, we are able to process emotions that would otherwise remain hidden. Acknowledging and dealing with these hidden emotions helps us avoid accumulations of stress and tension. But we can also reflect on experiences: meditating allows us to make sense of the past, helping us to understand what we have learned, and how we can apply these lessons in our future lives. That process of reflection can lead to greater self-awareness and personal growth. In addition, taking time to reflect helps us reconnect with our core values, ensuring that our actions are aligned with what we truly believe is important.

THE POWER OF CONTEMPLATION Allowing yourself regular time for deep contemplation can help you find peace and process change.

1. Find a quiet place. Make sure you are comfortable with a relaxed posture. If you wish, you can light a scented candle or use an essential oil diffuser.
2. Begin by closing your eyes and taking a few deep breaths. Inhale slowly through your nose, filling your lungs with air, and then exhale slowly through your mouth. Repeat this deep breathing cycle for 2–3 minutes.
3. Bring your attention to the present moment. Notice how you feel, both physically and emotionally. If your thoughts begin to wander, bring them back to the present. To do this, focus on your breathing or pulse.
4. Take a few minutes to reflect in silence. Think about recent changes in your life and how you feel about them. Let thoughts and emotions emerge naturally, without judgment.
5. After a few minutes, open your eyes and jot down your thoughts in your notebook or tablet. Note down some practical steps you can take to create regular times for reflection and quiet.

THE FIRST FROSTS OF AUTUMN

霜降

Sōkō

FIRST FROST BITES,
CRYSTAL SPARKLES,
FAREWELL FLOWERS.

OCTOBER 23–27

FROST BEGINS TO FORM

霜始降 *Shimo hajimete furu*

As the first frost transforms the landscape, let calm and reflection transform your spirit too, preparing you for new beginnings.

The first frost invites reflection and calm. When nature transforms under the ice, the environment becomes serene and contemplative. The stillness of a frozen landscape offers us the perfect opportunity to stop, reflect, and find inner peace.

The calm that comes from the first frost encourages us to slow our pace, reconsider our priorities, and connect with ourselves more deeply. Reflection allows us to process our thoughts and feelings, helping us to find clarity and make more thoughtful decisions.

But reflection also allows us to identify our priorities. During this period of introspection, we can effectively reconsider our goals. This gives us a chance to determine whether they are still aligned with our current values and desires. This is a time to make necessary adjustments and align our actions with our goals.

Reflecting on our past and present gives us the opportunity to plan our future with greater intention and purpose. We can create concrete strategies to achieve our goals, taking into account the lessons learned from our past experiences.

LEARNING TO STOP Use this exercise to help you find the stillness that will allow you to contemplate and prepare for changes in your life.

1. Create a peaceful environment or find a quiet place. Make sure you are comfortable with a relaxed posture.
2. Close your eyes and start taking a few deep breaths. Inhale through your nose, filling your lungs with air, and then exhale through your mouth. Repeat this deep breathing cycle for about 2–3 minutes, allowing your body and mind to relax completely.
3. Imagine yourself in a landscape covered by the first frost. Visualize the ephemeral beauty of the frost covering the grass and trees, creating a shimmering blanket beneath the first rays of the sun.
4. Think about the changes you are facing or expect to face in the near future. Reflect on how you feel about these changes and what you can do to best prepare yourself. Let the stillness of the frozen landscape help you find clarity and awareness.
5. Open your eyes and jot down your thoughts in your notebook or tablet, without judging.
6. Reflect on what is important to you. Note down your priorities to align your daily actions with your values and goals.

OCTOBER 28–NOVEMBER 1

LIGHT RAIN FALLS ON THE EARTH

霎時施 *Kosame tokidoki furu*

As light rains purify the earth, let calm and reflection purify your mind and spirit.

The *Kosame tokidoki furu* microseason marks the arrival of occasional light rains, a natural phenomenon that brings a sense of freshness and renewal to the land. These subtle, intermittent rains cleanse the air, nourishing the soil without the tumultuous effects of bigger storms. Their presence represents a gentle transition, preparing nature for the imminent winter, and instilling calm and serenity.

Light rains symbolize purification and renewal. They wash away dust and impurities, invigorating plants and the earth. Similarly, we can see these moments as an opportunity to purify our minds and spirits, ridding ourselves of negative thoughts and harmful habits. The gentle sound of falling raindrops brings with it a sense of tranquility. This serenity creates a perfect environment for reflection and meditation, inviting us to slow down and appreciate the quiet moments in our lives.

This microseason teaches us the importance of preparing for and adapting to change. Light rains prepare nature for winter, reminding us to be flexible and ready to accept new challenges and opportunities. Adaptability is a fundamental quality for coping with transitions in life. Just as nature adapts to seasonal changes, we too can learn to be more flexible and resilient. Accepting change as an integral part of life allows us to grow and develop in ways we never imagined.

Learning to slow down and appreciate quiet moments can significantly improve our quality of life. During this microseason, we can practice gratitude for small daily joys and find beauty in simple things. Inner calm allows us to face difficulties with greater tranquility and maintain a positive outlook, even in times of stress.

In conclusion, *Kosame tokidoki furu* is not just a period of light rain, but an opportunity to reflect, purify, and prepare for the future. Learning to slow down, appreciate calm moments, and adapt to change helps us develop greater resilience and a deeper understanding of ourselves. During this time, we can find inspiration in nature and apply the lessons it offers us to our daily lives, creating a space for personal growth and renewal.

MEDITATION ON LIGHT RAIN Through this rain-inspired meditation, you will find moments of calm and reflection, ridding yourself of negative thoughts and harmful habits. By learning to purify your mind and spirit, you can develop an awareness of yourself and your emotions, preparing the ground for continued personal growth and renewal.

1. Find a quiet place where you can sit comfortably without being disturbed. If you wish, you can use soothing background music to mimic the sound of light rain. Bring a notebook or tablet with you to record any reflections at the end of the meditation.
2. Create a relaxing environment. Sit in a quiet, comfortable place. Make sure your posture is relaxed but alert. If you wish, light a candle or use a relaxing essential oil in a diffuser to create a serene atmosphere.
3. Close your eyes and start to take a few deep breaths. Slowly inhale through your nose, filling your lungs with air, and then slowly exhale through your mouth. Repeat this cycle of deep breathing for about 2–3 minutes, allowing your body and mind to relax completely.
4. Imagine you are in a quiet place outdoors where a light rain is falling. Visualize the raindrops gently falling on the earth, purifying the air and nourishing the soil. Feel the freshness and serenity they bring.

5 Connect with the rain. Imagine that each raindrop represents a negative thought or emotion you want to let go of. Visualize the drops falling and dissolving into the earth, freeing your mind and spirit from all burdens.

6 As you continue to breathe deeply, reflect on what you wish to purify in your life. Gently bring your attention to the negative thoughts, harmful habits, or stressful situations that you would like to let go of. As you do so, visualize yourself becoming lighter and more serene, just as the earth is renewed by the light rain.

7 Feel the calmness that the light rain brings. Let this serenity envelop you completely. Take a moment to appreciate the tranquility and beauty of this moment. Allow yourself to be completely present, enjoying the inner peace you have created.

8 When you are ready, begin to slowly bring your attention back to the present. Gently move your fingers and toes, allowing your body to awaken. Slowly open your eyes and take a moment to orient yourself in your surroundings.

9 In your notebook or tablet, jot down your reflections. Write down everything that came up during your meditation, without judging or censoring yourself.

NOVEMBER 2–6

YELLOWING MAPLE AND IVY LEAVES

楓蔦黄 *Momiji tsuta kibamu*

When you accept the natural flow of life, you find peace in letting go and strength in starting over.

Momiji tsuta kibamu marks an enchanting moment in the Japanese autumn, when maple and ivy leaves begin to turn to beautiful shades of yellow. This color transformation represents one of nature's most striking spectacles and reminds us that change is an inevitable part of life, and that each stage has its own beauty and meaning. The transformation of the leaves can be seen as an invitation to celebrate the beauty of the present and to let go of what no longer serves us, be it habits, thoughts, or relationships that don't enrich us anymore, in order to pave the way for new experiences and growth.

This process is not only a biological necessity, but also a symbol of renewal. When trees drop their leaves, they conserve energy to survive the colder months; similarly, letting go in our lives means getting rid of what is harmful to make room for new opportunities and growth.

Reflecting on our habits and identifying those that no longer serve us improves our quality of life. Letting go of these habits creates space to develop new, healthier ones that will help us grow and thrive. Negative thoughts, for example, can be a huge burden, like dry leaves

weighing down the branches of a tree. Practices such as meditation, journal writing, and psychological therapy can be helpful in identifying and turning negative thoughts into positive ones.

LET GO OF WHAT NO LONGER SERVES YOU This exercise provides both space for reflection and a physical act to represent casting off negative aspects of your life. If possible, choose a time of day when you can devote at least 20–30 minutes to this exercise.

1. Find a place where you can sit without being disturbed. Take a notebook or tablet with you to jot down your thoughts as well as a sheet of paper and a pen. Make sure your posture is relaxed but alert. If you wish, light a candle or use an essential oil diffuser to create a serene atmosphere. Close your eyes and start taking a few deep breaths.
2. Imagine you are in an autumn forest, surrounded by maple and ivy trees. Visualize the leaves changing color and falling gently to the ground. Feel the calmness and beauty of this moment. Each falling leaf represents something you want to get rid of.
3. Think about those aspects of your life that no longer serve you. Reflect on habits, thoughts, relationships, or situations that you feel you need to let go of to make room for new opportunities and growth.
4. Open your eyes and jot down your thoughts and feelings in your notebook or tablet. Write down everything that came up during your reflection, without judging or censoring your reflections.
5. Take a sheet of paper and write a list of the things you want to get rid of. Once you have completed the list, read each item aloud and then tear the paper into small pieces. Imagine that, as you tear up the paper, you are freeing yourself from these burdens.

WINTER HAS BEGUN

立冬

Rittō

WINTER CALLS,
CRISP AIR EMBRACES,
SILENCE SPREADS.

NOVEMBER 7–11

THE CAMELLIAS BLOOM

山茶始開 *Tsubaki hajimete hiraku*

Find beauty in small things, even in moments of difficulty. That is where true strength lies.

Camellias, known in Japanese as *tsubaki*, are beloved for their elegance and resilience. They bloom in the winter months, lending vibrancy to landscapes with their petals. Their presence in winter encourages us to look for beauty in our daily lives, even when everything seems gray and hopeless. This requires a change of perspective, a conscious attention to the small moments of joy that often go unnoticed. Learning to see the beauty in the little things can transform the way we face dark times.

Camellias not only survive the winter, they thrive. This teaches us that we can find the strength to keep fighting and thriving despite adversity. The resilience of camellias inspires us not to give up in the face of difficulties, but to see challenges as opportunities for growth. This lesson is especially relevant in times of uncertainty and crisis.

The blossoming of camellias invites us to unearth valuable lessons and opportunities for personal development. Learning to dig deeper and see beyond immediate difficulties can reveal interior resources and new possibilities that can transform our lives.

FINDING BEAUTY IN THE LITTLE THINGS This exercise will help you develop the ability to find and appreciate beauty in the small things of your daily life. Learning to see the beauty in simple things can improve your well-being.

1. Sit down in a quiet, comfortable place. Close your eyes and begin to take a few deep breaths. Slowly inhale through your nose, filling your lungs with air, and then slowly exhale through your mouth.

Repeat this deep breathing cycle for about 2–3 minutes, allowing your body and mind to relax completely.

2. Open your eyes and look closely at your surroundings. Try to notice the small details that you might normally miss. It might be the light filtering through a window, the sound of leaves moving in the wind, or the texture of a piece of fabric.
3. Reflect on the beauty of small things. Take out your notebook or tablet and jot down at least five things you have noticed that seem beautiful or interesting to you.
4. Reflect on the daily activities that you often carry out without thinking about them. It might be drinking a cup of tea, walking to work, or preparing a meal. Try to find something beautiful or fulfilling in these activities. At the end of the day, take some time to reflect on what you experienced and write down three things in your notebook you are grateful for.

NOVEMBER 12–16

THE GROUND STARTS TO FREEZE

地始凍 *Chi hajimete kōru*

When silence embraces your heart, you discover your inner strength and prepare your spirit to grow and prosper.

The onset of frost invites us to enter a period of reflection and introspection, when we can look within and better understand ourselves, identifying what is truly important. The freezing of the earth can be seen as a metaphor for the need to consolidate and put our inner lives in order. Just as nature conserves energy during a period of frost, we too can learn to better manage our internal resources. This means taking care of ourselves and recharging our emotional and mental reserves, ensuring that we are ready to face future challenges. Instead of wasting our energy on activities that exhaust us, let us focus instead on what nourishes us.

During this period, we can reflect on past experiences and how they have shaped us. This process of introspection helps us identify desires and goals we feel are important. This time of frost invites us to breathe deeply and reconnect with ourselves. Through mindfulness practices we can cultivate a sense of calm and tranquility. Inner peace is not just the absence of conflict, but also a deep sense of harmony between ourselves and the world. Thus, the onset of frost allows us to conserve our energy and find inner peace so we are ready to blossom when spring arrives.

PREPARING FOR WINTER This meditation is inspired by the way nature conserves energy in winter, ready for next spring. Devote at least 30 minutes to this exercise.

1 Find a place where you can sit without being disturbed. Bring a notebook or tablet with you to jot down your reflections. If you wish, light a candle or use an essential oil diffuser to create a relaxing atmosphere. Close your eyes and begin to take a few deep breaths.

2 Think about the past few months and the experiences you have gone through. Reflect on what you have learned and how these experiences have shaped you. Record your reflections in your notebook or tablet.

3 Examine your current goals and desires. Assess whether they are still aligned with your values and aspirations. Note any changes or adjustments you wish to make.

4 Reflect on how you manage your internal resources. Think about how you can improve your energy management to be more balanced and less stressed.

5 Take time to practice mindfulness. Relax and let go of any tension. Focus on finding balance and inner peace.

An example of mindfulness practice:

- Sit comfortably and close your eyes.
- Bring your attention to your breath. Notice the air going in and out of your body.
- If your mind begins to wander, gently bring it back to the breath. Continue for 10–15 minutes, allowing any thoughts or emotions to pass without judgment.

NOVEMBER 17–21

THE DAFFODILS ARE IN FLOWER

金盞香 *Kinsenka saku*

Even on the coldest, darkest days, daffodils show us that beauty and hope can bloom anywhere.

In Japan, daffodils are prized for their elegance and ability to bloom in difficult conditions. These flowers are associated with hope and new life, symbolizing the capacity to find beauty even in the darkest moments. In Japanese culture, daffodils are also a symbol of good luck and prosperity; they are often grown in gardens and used in flower arrangements to decorate homes during autumn and winter.

The ability of daffodils to bloom in cold, dark conditions is a powerful metaphor for the beauty and strength that can emerge even in the face of challenges. These flowers not only survive but thrive at a time of year when many plants are dormant, demonstrating extraordinary resilience.

Daffodils encourage us to look deeper, to seek out those moments of beauty that can lift our spirits and give us the strength to move forward. They are also an invitation to slow down and notice the small details, such as the simple beauty of a flower blossoming in the frost.

To cultivate a mindset of beauty, we practice gratitude and mindfulness. Gratitude makes us focus on what is positive, even when everything seems difficult. Mindfulness allows us to notice the little things that often go unnoticed.

MAKING EVERYDAY DETAILS COUNT This exercise will help you develop the ability to find and appreciate beauty in the small details of daily life, even in times of difficulty.

1. Find a place where you can sit without being disturbed. Bring a notebook or tablet with you. If you wish, light a candle or use an essential oil diffuser to create a relaxing atmosphere. Close your eyes and begin to take a few deep breaths. Inhale slowly through your nose, filling your lungs with air, and then exhale slowly through your mouth. Repeat this deep breathing cycle for about 2–3 minutes.
2. Open your eyes and look closely at your surroundings. Try to notice the small details that often go unnoticed. It can be anything: the texture of a leaf, the sound of a bird, sunlight filtering through a window, or even an everyday object.
3. Take your notebook or tablet and spend a few minutes writing a brief description of the beautiful things you noticed. Try to be as detailed as possible, describing not only the visual aspect, but also the feelings and emotions these details evoke in you.
4. Think about a recent challenge you have faced. Reflect on how, despite the difficulty, you were able to find moments of beauty or joy. Jot down your reflections in your notebook.
5. Commit to finding a moment each day to observe and appreciate the beauty in small things. It can be a morning ritual of observation, a mindful walk, or simply taking a moment during the day to notice something beautiful.

FIRST SNOW WHITENS THE GROUND

小雪

Shōsetsu

LIGHT FLAKES,
SILENT DANCE,
I WANT TO REST.

NOVEMBER 22–26

RAINBOWS HIDE IN GRAY SKY

虹蔵不見 *Niji kakurete miezu*

Beauty does not disappear. Instead, it hides only to be rediscovered with new eyes.

The microseason *Niji kakurete miezu* invites us to cultivate hope even when there are no visible signs of improvement. Rainbows, which appear after rain, are symbols of hope and new beginnings. But during this microseason, rainbows are rarer due to the changes in weather as winter approaches. This phenomenon teaches us that even when circumstances seem gray and difficult, hope can be hidden but still present.

Hope is a force that can give us the courage to face challenges and the motivation to keep going. In hard times, it is easy to feel overwhelmed and lose sight of the possibility of a better future. However, like the rainbow that only appears when the conditions are right, cultivating hope helps us maintain an optimistic outlook and have faith that difficult times will pass, bringing with them new possibilities and beauty.

Keeping hope alive, even in the darkest of times, is essential for our emotional and mental well-being. But seeing possibilities and opportunities even when they are not immediately visible is an active choice, enabling us to face adversity with a positive and resilient mindset.

JOURNAL OF HOPE Develop and keep hope alive by recording small joys, positive thoughts, and moments of gratitude on a daily basis.

1. At the end of each day, use your journal to record and reflect on the day's events. Try to focus on the positive moments, the small joys, and anything that made you smile or gave you hope.
2. Write in your journal three positive things you experienced during the day. These can be moments of gratitude, personal accomplishments, or simply beauties of nature that you noticed.

3 Take a few minutes to think about the future and note in your journal your aims and aspirations. This can include short-term goals, long-term dreams, or simply hopes for a better tomorrow.

4 Periodically, re-read what you have written in your hope journal. This will help you see how much you have accomplished, remember the good times, and maintain an optimistic outlook, even during difficult moments.

NOVEMBER 27–DECEMBER 1

THE NORTH WIND TAKES THE LEAVES

朔風払葉 *Kitakaze konoha o harau*

Let go of what is holding you back, open your heart to new possibilities, and embrace change with confidence.

The north wind that blows away the dead leaves is a symbol of renewal and purification as well as a valuable lesson in letting go of what no longer serves us in our lives, creating space for new beginnings. Just as the north wind takes the leaves from the trees, so we must learn to cast aside these harmful habits to make room for new, healthier, and more productive practices.

LET GO OF NEGATIVE THOUGHTS

Negative thoughts are often the main obstacles to our mental and emotional well-being. Whenever there is self-doubt, irrational fears, or regrets about the past, the north wind reminds us that we can choose to rid our minds of these toxic thoughts.

STEP AWAY FROM UNCONSTRUCTIVE RELATIONSHIPS

Not all relationships are meant to last forever, and some can become toxic or unsustainable. Ending relationships that no longer enrich us is a difficult but necessary step.

CREATING SPACE FOR NEW BEGINNINGS

Letting go is not only an act of elimination, but also an act of creation. By eliminating what is no longer needed, we create space for new beginnings.

PERSONAL GROWTH

Personal growth requires a constant process of renewal and adaptation. Just as trees lose their leaves in preparation for spring, we too must choose to let go of the old to make room for the new.

CREATING SPACE This exercise is designed to help you reflect on what you need to let go, releasing negativity and making room in your life for future growth.

1. Find a quiet place where you can sit without being disturbed. Bring a notebook or tablet with you to jot down your reflections. If you wish, light a candle or use an essential oil diffuser to create a relaxing atmosphere. Close your eyes and take a few deep breaths.
2. Think about the aspects of your life you need to let go of. This may include habits, thoughts, emotions, or relationships that no longer serve you. Reflect on how they affect you and how releasing them might improve your well-being.
3. Write down in your notebook or tablet all the things you wish to let go of. Be specific and honest with yourself. This act of writing helps to create the intention for release.
4. Close your eyes and imagine a cold wind blowing away all the items on your list. Visualize the wind taking the dead leaves, ridding you of burdens and creating space for new beginnings.

DECEMBER 2–6

THE TACHIBANA LEAVES TURN YELLOW

橘始黄 *Tachibana hajimete kibamu*

Embrace change with serenity, knowing that each closing chapter opens a new one.

In Japan, the tachibana, a type of mandarin orange, is a symbol of longevity and good luck. Its presence in many homes during the winter symbolizes health and prosperity. Its yellowing leaves are not only a sign of the changing seasons, but also a reminder of the beauty of transition and the importance of adapting to natural cycles.

The changing leaves offer us a vivid image of the cyclical nature of life. In nature, change is a constant, an ongoing process that ensures growth and renewal. When we observe the tachibana leaves turning yellow, we witness a transition: a shift from the lush energy of summer to the preparatory calm of winter. This is not just a visual transformation, but a signal that the tree is conserving energy to survive the cold months and regenerate in the following spring.

This phenomenon also teaches us the importance of adapting to new circumstances. When leaves change color and fall, the tree does not lose its essence; it prepares for a new phase of growth. Similarly, accepting changes in our lives allows us to adapt and continue to grow. Adapting does not mean giving up our goals or values, but finding new ways to pursue them in a different context.

Just like the tachibana tree preparing for spring during the winter months, we too can use periods of change to reflect, reorganize, and plan for our future with renewed determination.

PREPARING FOR NEW BEGINNINGS This meditation will assist you in embracing the effects of change and inspire you to welcome change as a positive force.

1. Find a quiet place where you can sit without being disturbed. Bring a notebook or tablet with you to jot down your reflections. If you wish, light a candle or use an essential oil diffuser to create a relaxing atmosphere. Close your eyes and take a few deep and calming breaths.
2. Think about recent changes in your life, both positive and challenging. Reflect on how these changes have affected you.
3. Jot down in your notebook or tablet the new beginnings you want to undertake. These can be personal goals, professional projects, or changes in your habits. Be specific and detailed. Think about moments of transition in your life and try to identify their beauty and significance. Record your reflections as well.
4. Close your eyes and imagine yourself embarking on the new beginnings you have identified. Visualize yourself accomplishing your goals and feel the satisfaction and joy that comes from achieving your desires.

THICK SNOW FALLS

大雪

Taisetsu

SLOW DOWN,
IN THE SOFT SILENCE,
I FALL ASLEEP.

DECEMBER 7–11

COLD WEATHER ARRIVES, WINTER BEGINS

閉塞成冬 *Sora samuku fuyu to naru*

Inner calm is the key to facing life's challenges with serenity and determination.

Winter, with its shorter days and cold temperatures, teaches us the importance of acceptance and flexibility. This time of year requires a different approach to daily life, as weather conditions affect not only our external environment, but also our inner well-being. Shorter days and reduced access to sunlight can impact our mood and energy levels, making it essential to adopt strategies to maintain balance and serenity. Accepting and adapting to changing weather conditions requires patience and flexibility.

PHYSICAL AND MENTAL PREPARATION

Adapting to winter involves not only the inevitable physical challenges, but the mental and emotional challenges too. Preparing mentally for winter means developing a positive and resilient mindset. This may mean finding ways to enjoy winter activities, such as walking in nature, reading engaging books, or practicing hobbies that bring joy and satisfaction. It is important to recognize and accept your limits, avoiding overloading yourself, and allow yourself moments of rest and reflection.

Mental preparation can also include the practice of mindfulness, which helps maintain calmness and focus. Mindfulness allows us to be present in the moment, accepting it without judgment. This practice can be especially helpful during winter, when darker, colder days can induce feelings of isolation or sadness. Being aware of your feelings and accepting them with kindness helps you better navigate emotional challenges.

OPPORTUNITIES FOR GROWTH

Accepting that some phases of life require more patience allows us to live with greater peace of mind. Each season, with its unique characteristics, offers opportunities that we can make the most of if we consciously adapt. Winter, with its slower pace, invites us to re-evaluate our priorities and set new goals with a sense of calm and determination. The natural slowdown of winter is an opportunity to reflect on what is important to us. We can use this time to take stock of our lives, identify what we want to change or improve, and plan how to achieve our goals. This process of reflection and planning can lead us to greater clarity and direction, preparing us for the more active months ahead.

ADAPTABILITY

Winter teaches us the importance of adaptability. Changing conditions require us to be flexible in our approach and ready to modify our plans in response to shifting circumstances. This adaptability is crucial not only during winter, but at all stages of life. Being adaptable enables us to cope better with uncertainty and change, turning potential obstacles into opportunities for growth. Accepting and adapting to the challenges of winter teaches us valuable lessons that we can apply to every aspect of our lives.

DEVELOPING PATIENCE This meditative practice will guide you through a process of introspection and relaxation, helping you to develop patience and find inner serenity.

1 Sit comfortably in a place where you will not be disturbed. Wear comfortable clothes and, if necessary, cover yourself with a blanket to stay warm. Breathe deeply: close your eyes and start to take deep, slow breaths. Inhale through your nose, filling your lungs, and exhale through your mouth, slowly releasing the air.

2 Bring your attention to your breath. Feel the air move in and out of your nose. Notice how the breath moves in and out of your body, without forcing it. Let your breath become natural and relaxed.

3 Imagine you are in a peaceful winter landscape. Visualize the snow slowly falling and covering the ground, creating a soft, white blanket. Feel the cool, crisp air on your face and listen to the silence that accompanies winter. Allow this scene to fill your mind and body with calm and tranquility.

4 Think about nature in winter. Trees are bare, plants rest, and animals conserve energy. Everything in nature takes its time to prepare for spring rebirth. Recognize how this patience and rest are essential for growth and new awakenings.

5 Reflect on how you can incorporate patience into your daily life. Think of situations in which you could be more patient with yourself and others. Visualize yourself approaching these situations calmly and serenely, accepting that everything has its time.

6 Mentally repeat some affirmations that help you develop patience. For example, "I accept that everything has its own time" or "I trust in the natural process of life."

7 When you feel ready, slowly bring your attention to the present. Become aware of your body, whether you are sitting or lying down, and listen to the sounds around you. Take a few deep breaths and, when you are ready, slowly open your eyes.

8 Take a few moments to reflect on how you feel after this meditation. Take the feeling of calmness and patience with you into the rest of your day. Remember that, like nature in winter, you too can find strength and beauty in patience and rest.

DECEMBER 12–16

BEARS RETREAT INTO HIBERNATION

熊蟄穴 *Kuma ana ni komoru*

Rest is not a luxury, but a fundamental necessity for well-being and personal growth.

Hibernating bears offer us a metaphor for the importance of rest and regeneration. In a world increasingly dominated by urgency and constant connectedness, we often ignore the need to take time to rest and recuperate. However, the hibernation of bears teaches us that rest is not a luxury, but a basic necessity for our physical and mental well-being. In fact, this period of deep rest is essential for their survival and allows them to prepare for spring rebirth.

During hibernation, bears slow their metabolism, saving energy and allowing their bodies to heal and regenerate. Similarly, for humans, periods of rest and adequate sleep are essential for tissue repair, strengthening the immune system, and muscle recovery. Rest allows our bodies to release growth hormones and repair any cellular damage.

On a mental level, rest helps memory and cognitive function. During sleep, the brain processes information gathered during the day, facilitating learning and creativity. Without adequate rest, our cognitive and decision-making abilities are impaired, which increases the risk of errors and accidents.

REGENERATION AND GROWTH

Despite their apparent state of inactivity, bears accumulate energy reserves during the long months of hibernation. This process teaches us that rest is an opportunity to accumulate internal resources, preparing us to face future challenges with renewed strength and determination. For humans, periods of rest can be opportunities to reflect on past experiences, recharge our energy, and plan new goals.

REST AND PRODUCTIVITY

Studies show that taking regular breaks can increase both productivity and creativity. Rest allows us to avoid burnout, maintain consistent energy levels, and improve our concentration. Taking time to rest makes us more efficient.

REST AND EMOTIONAL WELL-BEING

Rest also has an impact on our mental well-being. Lack of sleep and rest breaks can lead to irritability, stress, and mental health problems such as anxiety and depression. Resting or relaxing can improve mood, reducing stress and emotional instability.

STRATEGIES FOR INTEGRATING REST INTO DAILY LIFE

To integrate rest into our daily lives, we can adopt several strategies: a regular sleep routine, going to bed and waking up at the same time each day; taking short breaks during the workday; devoting time to relaxation with meditation, reading, or hot baths; limiting the use of electronic devices before sleep; and creating a noise- and distraction-free environment that promotes sleep.

This exercise is designed to help you integrate rest and regeneration into your daily routine, taking inspiration from animal hibernation. The goal is to recognize the importance of rest for your physical and mental health and to adopt habits that promote recovery and resilience.

1. Find a quiet place where you can sit comfortably and not be disturbed. You can sit in a chair, on a meditation cushion, or lie down.
2. Bring your attention to your breath. Feel the air enter and leave your body through your nose. Let your breathing become natural and calm. Imagine you are a bear preparing for hibernation, feeling your body relax deeply.

3 Think about times in your life when you have neglected rest, perhaps because you felt too busy. Reflect on how this has affected your physical and mental health. Record in your mind or in a notebook or tablet the impact a lack of rest has on you.

4 Identify activities and habits that help you relax and recharge. Note down the things that bring you calm and serenity.

5 Plan how you can incorporate more rest into your daily routine. Note down specific actions you can take to make sure you have time to rest and rejuvenate.

6 Visualize yourself practicing these new rest habits. Imagine going to bed at the same time each night, taking regular breaks throughout the day, and spending time on activities that recharge you. Imagine how these habits will improve your overall well-being and prepare you to face future challenges with renewed energy.

7 When you feel ready, slowly and gently bring your attention to the present. Become aware of your body, whether you are sitting or lying down, and listen to the sounds around you. Take a few deep breaths and, when you are ready, slowly open your eyes.

DECEMBER 17–21

SCHOOLS OF SALMON BRAVE THE CURRENT

鱖魚群 *Sake no uo muragaru*

Strength is not measured by the calm waters you cross, but by the currents you can swim against.

The difficult journey of salmon against the current is an extraordinary example of perseverance and determination. These fish make an epic journey, often hundreds of miles long, facing currents, natural obstacles, and predators. Despite these difficulties, they continue to push toward their goal: to reach their spawning grounds and lay their eggs.

The perseverance of salmon teaches us a fundamental lesson: to face adversity with courage. At every stage of their journey, salmon show great determination in overcoming difficulties. Even when currents are particularly strong, or they have to jump over huge waterfalls, salmon do not give up. This tenacity is an example of how, with concentration and focus, we too can overcome the obstacles we encounter in life.

The perseverance of the salmon teaches us that courage is not the absence of fear, but rather it is keeping going despite difficulties. Salmon do not stop in the face of obstacles; they face them with an inner strength that drives them to continue their journey. This reminds us that we can find the courage within ourselves to face challenges, even the most insurmountable ones.

The ability of these fish to overcome setbacks is inspiring. Every jump they make, every current they face, represents a step toward their goal. This shows us that with the right mindset and dedication, we can overcome any obstacle. Every small step forward is progress toward success.

The salmons' determination to overcome adversity also teaches us that success is not just the end result, but also the journey and the sacrifices we make along the way. Each challenge we face makes us stronger and brings us closer to our goals.

The salmons' journey to their spawning grounds is also a powerful reminder of our origins. These fish make an extraordinary, often long and perilous journey back to the rivers and streams where they were born. This return to their origins is essential for their survival and for the continuation of the species. Their journey symbolizes the cyclical nature of life and a deep connection to their roots.

The example provided by the salmon invites us to reflect on the importance of getting back to basics. In our busy and often chaotic lives, it is easy to lose sight of what is truly important. Rediscovering our roots, values, and traditions can give us a solid foundation on which to build our existence.

Maintaining a connection to our own roots is essential for our emotional and spiritual well-being. Roots represent our history, our experiences, and the people who have contributed to shaping us. This connection provides us with a sense of belonging and identity, reminding us of who we are and where we came from. The return of salmon to their origins also represents the cycle of life and continuity. The cyclical nature of life reminds us that each ending brings with it a new beginning. Acknowledging and accepting this cyclicality allows us to face changes with greater serenity and confidence.

PERSEVERANCE AND RESILIENCE This exercise will help you develop perseverance and resilience, inspiring you through the journey of the salmon against the current. The goal is to recognize your challenges, find the inner strength to face them, and rediscover what is truly important to you.

1 Find a quiet place where you can sit comfortably without being disturbed. Bring a notebook or tablet with you to jot down your reflections.

2. Create a relaxing environment. If you wish, light a candle or use an essential oil diffuser to create a relaxing atmosphere. Close your eyes and take a few deep breaths to fully relax.
3. Bring your attention to your breath. Feel the air enter and leave your nose. Let your breathing become natural and relaxed.
4. Think about the current challenges in your life. Visualize these challenges as strong currents trying to hold you back. Record in your mind or in a notebook or tablet the specific challenges you are facing.
5. Visualize yourself facing these currents with strength and determination, just like the salmon. Think about the inner qualities and resources that help you overcome difficulties. Note down your inner resources.
6. Reflect on your values, your roots, and what is important to you. Visualize yourself returning to the basics, just as salmon return to their birthplaces. Note down your core values.
7. Visualize yourself achieving your goals, despite facing difficulties. Imagine the feeling of success and accomplishment when you overcome challenges. Feel how this visualization motivates you to keep pushing forward.
8. When you feel ready, slowly bring your attention to the present. Become aware of your body, whether you are sitting or lying down, and listen to the sounds around you. Take a few deep breaths and, when you are ready, slowly open your eyes.

THE WINTER SOLSTICE
冬至
Tōji
TIME PASSES,
NIGHT EMBRACES
THE SKY,
I STAY HOME.

DECEMBER 22–26

THE SHOOTS OF SELF-HEAL APPEAR

乃東生 *Natsukarekusa shōzu*

Every challenge faced with courage is an opportunity to discover our inner strength and to grow.

In many cultures, including Japan's, the plant known as Asian self-heal (*Prunella vulgaris* subsp. *asiatica*) is considered a symbol of strength and regeneration. The appearance of its shoots during winter is seen as a sign of hope and continuity, reminding us that life persists despite climatic difficulties. This flower teaches us that life continues even in the harshest and most hostile times. Self-heal does not wait for ideal conditions to start growing, but germinates in the depths of winter.

THE IMPORTANCE OF PERSISTENCE

Persistence is the ability to keep advancing toward our goals despite difficulties and obstacles. Difficulties should not stop us but instead motivate us. Self-heal sprouts in winter, when most plants are dormant, teaching us that it is possible to find the strength to grow even in the most adverse circumstances.

PATIENCE AND PERSEVERANCE

Self-heal also teaches us the importance of patience. Reflecting its slow growth and preparation for spring, we too must have patience in pursuing our goals. Perseverance enables us to keep working toward our aims, even when the results are not immediately visible.

CULTIVATE RESILIENCE AND PATIENCE This exercise will help you develop resilience and patience, inspired by the self-heal shoots that appear during winter.

1. Close your eyes and start to take deep breaths. Inhale gently through your nose, filling your lungs with air, and then exhale through your mouth. Repeat for 2–3 minutes.
2. In a notebook or tablet, write a list of the challenges you are currently facing.
3. Next to the challenges, write down the resources you have at your disposal for dealing with them. Think of qualities such as patience, determination, resilience, or the support of loved ones.
4. Close your eyes again and visualize yourself facing and overcoming these difficulties. Imagine yourself as the self-heal sending up shoots in the cold, finding the strength to grow despite adversity.
5. Create a personal mantra that expresses your determination to succeed and resilience. Repeat this to yourself as you continue to breathe deeply.
6. When you feel ready, slowly bring your attention to the present. Become aware of your body, whether you are sitting or lying down, and listen to the sounds around you. Take a few deep breaths and, when you are ready, slowly open your eyes.

DECEMBER 27–31

DEER SHED THEIR ANTLERS

麋角解 *Sawashika no tsuno otsuru*

Change may be difficult, but it is through shifting circumstances that we find our true strength and are able to grow.

Change is often accompanied by a sense of uncertainty and discomfort. This is natural, as stepping out of our comfort zone can be frightening and disorienting. However, it is only through these changes that we can find our inner strength and grow as individuals. The microseason *Sawashika no tsuno otsuru*, in which deer shed their antlers, offers a powerful metaphor for this process.

Just as deer adapt each year to the loss of their antlers to make room for the growth of new and stronger ones, so we can learn to adapt to new circumstances and find new opportunities for growth. This process requires courage and self-confidence, but it also enables us to become stronger and more capable of meeting future challenges.

Uncertainty is an inevitable part of life. Each day can present new challenges and unexpected changes. Learning to accept this helps us to live with greater serenity. Instead of resisting change, we can welcome new situations with an open mind, seeing them as opportunities to learn and grow. Of course, facing the unknown requires courage and self-confidence. Just like deer who face the loss of their antlers each year, so we must believe in our ability to adapt and thrive. Self-confidence is essential in order to face uncertainty with strength and resilience. Believing in ourselves is a foundational quality that enables us to face challenges with determination and to see difficulties as opportunities for growth rather than as insurmountable obstacles.

Confidence in one's own abilities is especially important when we are faced with difficult situations. Believing in oneself helps us to stay calm even in the most stressful situations. When we trust in our abilities, we are able to face challenges with a clear and focused mind, without being overwhelmed by anxiety or panic. Believing in ourselves also enables us to make thoughtful decisions even under pressure. Knowing that we can rely on our own expertise and judgment facilitates decision-making, reduces uncertainty, and encourages us to keep fighting, even when things get tough.

Being confident in our skills and potential allows us to approach new situations with an open and proactive mindset, seeing change as an opportunity rather than a threat.

DEVELOPING SELF-CONFIDENCE Self-confidence is an essential quality that enables us to face challenges with determination and serenity. This exercise is designed to help you develop and strengthen confidence in your abilities through reflection and action.

Reflect on past successes:

- Find a quiet place where you feel comfortable and there are no distractions. Take a notebook or tablet with you.
- Take a few minutes to reflect on the successes you have achieved in your life, whether big or small. Think of times when you overcame challenges, achieved important goals, or made significant progress.
- Write down your successes. List at least five achievements of which you are particularly proud, briefly describe what you did to achieve that success, and what personal qualities helped you.

Identify your strengths:

- Analyze your successes. Review your list and identify the qualities and skills you demonstrated in each case such as determination, creativity, or problem-solving skills.
- Write down your strengths. List these qualities and skills on another page. This is your list of strengths, which you can use as a reminder of your abilities.

Set realistic goals:

- Think of a realistic goal that you would like to achieve over the coming weeks or months. Make sure that this is specific, measurable, achievable, relevant, and time-bound (SMART).
- Plan your actions. Break down the goal into smaller, manageable steps. Write a detailed action plan that includes the steps required to achieve the goal, the resources you need, and a timeline for each step.

Practice self-compassion:

- Treat failures with kindness. Reflect on any difficulties you have recently encountered. Instead of judging yourself severely, try to see these events as learning opportunities.
- Write a message of self-compassion. Imagine writing a letter to a friend who has faced the same difficulties. Write a kind and encouraging message that offers support and understanding. Then, re-read the letter with yourself in mind as the recipient.

Take action:

- Start working on the steps in your action plan to achieve your goal. Use your list of strengths as a source of motivation and confidence.
- Monitor your progress. Keep track of the results you achieve. Each time you complete a step in your plan, note that success and reflect on how your personal qualities have helped you.

JANUARY 1–4

WHEAT SPROUTS BENEATH THE SNOW

雪下出麦 *Yuki watarite mugi nobiru*

Courage is manifested when you find the strength to grow, despite the frost that surrounds you.

In Japan, wheat is a symbol of abundance, fertility, and hope. Its ability to appear beneath the snow is a sign of promise and rebirth, indicating that even in the most difficult times, life continues to find ways to thrive. This time of year invites reflection on inner strength and the ability to grow despite challenges.

HOPE AND RENEWAL

The phenomenon of shoots emerging under the snow is a powerful metaphor for hope and renewal. Even when the outside world seems static and still, life continues to grow and develop beneath the surface. This teaches us that change and growth occur even at times when everything seems still and unaltered.

HOPE IN TIMES OF STAGNATION

Often in our lives, we find ourselves in situations where it seems as if nothing is changing. These moments can be frustrating and can make us feel stuck. However, the wheat growing under the snow reminds us that even during these periods of apparent stagnation, there is the possibility of renewal. Hope is the light that guides us through difficult times, helping us to see beyond immediate circumstances and believe in a better future.

SILENT RENEWAL

The process of growth under the snow is silent and hidden from view, but it is crucial to future development. It teaches us that renewal does not always have to be visible or dramatic. Often, the most significant changes occur below the surface, away from the eyes of the world. This kind of renewal requires patience and trust in the natural process of life.

THE POWER OF PATIENCE

The ability to maintain hope and believe in renewal requires patience. Grain does not sprout immediately, but goes through a slow and steady process. Learning to be patient and respect nature's timing allows us to cultivate resilience and inner strength. Patience is a virtue that helps us navigate challenges with serenity, knowing that each phase of difficulty brings with it the seed of growth.

TURN ADVERSITY INTO OPPORTUNITY

Shoots emerging from under the snow are a testimony to turning adversity into opportunity. Difficult conditions need not hinder growth, but can instead become the fertile ground from which new possibilities emerge. This invites us to see obstacles as opportunities for transformation and to look for ways to grow and improve, even when circumstances appear adverse.

CULTIVATE HOPE This exercise is designed to help you cultivate hope at times when you are experiencing the doldrums. Through meditation and practice, you will learn to see beyond present difficulties and recognize opportunities for growth and transformation.

Reflect on times of stagnation:

- Find a quiet place where you feel comfortable and there are no distractions. Take a notebook or tablet with you.
- Reflect on a period of stagnation you have gone through. Think of a time in your life when you felt stuck or when it seemed as if nothing was changing. Take a few minutes to visualize this experience and any associated feelings.
- Identify signs of growth. Write down at least three signs of positive change that emerged from the period of stasis you identified. Think about how these experiences helped you grow and evolve.

Visualize your growth:

- Close your eyes and imagine that you are a wheat seedling under the snow. Feel the protection and nourishment of the earth around you, even though everything above you seems still and cold.

- Imagine breaking through the earth. Visualize yourself growing slowly but steadily toward the surface, pushing through the snow and emerging into the light. Imagine how this growth brings strength and renewal to your life.
- Write down your thoughts. Note down the feelings you had during the visualization. Reflect on how this teaching applies to your current life and any challenges you are facing.

Plan for new beginnings:

- Define a new beginning. Think of an area in your life where you desire positive change or a new beginning. Note this desire as a specific goal.
- Break the goal down into steps. Divide your goal into small, manageable subgoals. Write an action plan that describes the actions needed to achieve this goal, the resources you need, and create a timetable for each of these steps.
- Monitor your progress. Keep track of the results you achieve. Each time you complete a step in the plan, note your success and reflect on how you feel.

Practice patience:

- Set a daily reminder to take a moment of calm and meditation. During this time, remember the wheat shoots growing under the snow and the need for patience.
- Practice a short patience meditation by concentrating on the breath. Inhale deeply and, as you exhale, imagine yourself cultivating patience. Repeat for 5 minutes, focusing on calmness and slow but steady growth.

COLD ENVELOPS THE WORLD

小寒

Shōkan

FAINT STARS,
LONG NIGHT WHISPERS
SILENCE.

JANUARY 5–9

THE PARSLEY FLOURISHES

芹乃栄 *Seri sunawachi sakau*

In the most difficult times you can discover your inner strength and bloom in all your splendor.

At a time of year when many plants are dormant, parsley not only survives but flourishes, demonstrating extraordinary adaptability and resilience. This inner strength is an essential quality for overcoming adversity and facing life's challenges with determination.

Inner strength refers to the ability to maintain calm and continue to persevere even in the face of difficulties. It is what enables us to face challenges with courage and not give up when things become difficult. Like the parsley that flourishes despite the cold, we too can find within ourselves the strength we need to overcome adversity. This strength helps us to focus on our goals and to keep fighting for what is important, even when everything seems to be going against us. Determination is the will to keep moving forward, despite obstacles. It is the ability to follow our goals and not let difficulties stop us. The flowering of parsley in winter is a perfect example of determination. Despite difficult conditions, the plant continues to grow and flourish, showing that with the right mindset and dedication, we can overcome any obstacle.

Overcoming adversity makes us stronger. Every time we face and overcome a difficulty, we learn something new about ourselves and about the world around us. This knowledge helps us grow and become more resilient. The parsley that blooms in winter teaches us that we can emerge from difficulties not just by surviving, but by thriving.

THE RESILIENCE MAP This exercise is designed to help you build a map of your inner resources, enabling you to better focus your energy on future challenges.

1 Find a quiet place where you feel comfortable and there are no distractions. Take a notebook or tablet with you.

2 Think about a current challenge you are facing. Take a few minutes to visualize this experience and its associated feelings.

3 Identify and write down at least three internal resources that you can use to address this challenge. Think of qualities such as patience, determination, and creativity. Also consider external resources, such as social support.

4 Draw your map. Start by drawing a large circle in the center of the page. Inside the circle, write your name.

5 Identify the roots of your strength. Around the circle, draw several roots extending outward. On each root, write an internal (or external) resource or quality that gives you strength and resilience.

6 Draw small shoots emerging from the roots, representing the ways in which these resources help you grow and overcome challenges. Write these next to the shoots.

JANUARY 10–14

THE ICE STARTS TO THAW

水泉動 *Shimizu atataka o fukumu*

Let go of what is keeping you trapped in a life you no longer want. Only then can you flow freely into new opportunities.

This microseason marks a period of transformation at the heart of winter. During this time, frozen springs and rivers begin to melt, allowing water to flow anew. This natural phenomenon offers a powerful metaphor for change and renewal in our lives. Just like the spring water breaking free from the winter frost, we too can find new energy and opportunities by welcoming change rather than resisting it.

ACCEPTING CHANGE

Accepting change is the first step toward growth. When we are faced with new or unexpected situations, our natural reaction may be one of resistance, as change can bring with it uncertainties and challenges. However, understanding that change is an integral part of life allows us to face it with an open mind and a positive attitude. Just like water flowing freely once the ice has melted, accepting change frees us from rigidities and fears, allowing us to flow into new possibilities.

ADAPTING TO CHANGES

Nature shows us that adaptability and flexibility are keys to survival and success. When springs thaw, water finds new paths, adapting easily to the surrounding terrain. Similarly, we must be ready to modify our plans in the face of new circumstances. Adaptability enables us to find creative solutions and make the most of opportunities.

GROWTH THROUGH CHANGE

Through the process of adaptation and acceptance, we develop new skills, as well as improve our resilience and our understanding of ourselves and the world around us. The difficulties and challenges associated with change force us out of our comfort zone and make us explore new horizons.

THE CYCLICAL NATURE OF LIFE

Just as springs thaw each year with the arrival of spring, we too go through cycles of change and renewal. Recognizing and accepting this cycle helps us to see change not as an end, but as a transitional phase that brings with it new opportunities. Each cycle of change offers us the chance to begin again and to grow.

REBIRTH AND RENEWAL

The melting of the ice in the springs marks a moment of transformation, in which what was frozen flows again, symbolizing the return of life. This phenomenon reminds us that even the most frozen situations can change and evolve, as well as signaling to us the importance of patience and trust in the transformation process. Just like water flowing after frost, we too can find new energy after periods of stagnation. The melting of ice symbolizes the release of tensions and blockages. It is an invitation to let go of what is holding us down, allowing us to flow freely into new opportunities.

RETURNING TO FLOW This guided meditation will help you reflect on accepting change, inspired by the natural process of thawing springs and rivers. Find a quiet place where you can sit comfortably and without distractions.

1. Find your inner calm. Sit in a comfortable position, with your back straight but relaxed. Close your eyes and bring your attention to your breath.
2. Inhale deeply through your nose for four seconds, hold for four seconds, and exhale slowly through your mouth for four seconds. Repeat this sequence three times, allowing your body and mind to relax.
3. Visualize the following:
    - Imagine you are in a winter landscape. Ahead of you, there is a frozen spring. The air is cold and everything seems still.
    - Observe this frozen spring, feeling the silence and stillness surrounding it.
    - Now, imagine that slowly, with the warmth of the sun, the ice begins to melt. You see small drops of water beginning to form and flow over the surface of the ice.
    - Visualize the thawing process gradually accelerating. The water begins to flow freely, filling the spring and invigorating the surrounding land.
    - Feel how the environment around you begins to transform, becoming more alive and vibrant with each passing drop.
    - Think of a situation in your life where you are facing a change. Visualize this change as ice melting in the spring.
    - Allow yourself to feel any emotions associated with this change, whether this is fear, anxiety, or resistance. Acknowledge these emotions without judging them.

- Imagine now that you welcome this change, just as the earth welcomes the water flowing from the spring. Feel how this acceptance frees you, allowing your mind and heart to open to new possibilities.
- Repeat to yourself, "I welcome change with openness and trust. I know that, like thawing springs, I can find new ways and new opportunities."

4. Slowly bring your attention to your breath. Inhale deeply and then exhale, letting go of any residual tension. When you feel ready, slowly open your eyes again. Take a few moments to gather yourself and return completely to the present.
5. Carry this feeling of openness and acceptance with you as you face changes in your daily life.

JANUARY 15–19

THE PHEASANTS START TO CALL

雉始雊 *Kiji hajimete naku*

Every day is an opportunity to express yourself; don't be afraid to make your voice heard.

This microseason marks the time when pheasants begin to make their distinctive calls. These birds, known for their bright colors and elegant plumage, are a symbol often associated with the Shinto goddess Amaterasu, the sun goddess. In many Japanese legends, the pheasant appears as a divine messenger, linking the world of humans with that of the gods.

The call of the pheasants reminds us to find and use our voice. This does not simply mean speaking, but authentically expressing who we are, including our feelings and ideas. In daily life, we often hold back from saying what we really think or feel, fearing judgment or rejection.

Pheasants make their calls to communicate their presence and mark their territory. Being authentic means expressing emotions, thoughts, and desires without filters. The courage to be authentic can lead to more sincere relationships, as people around us can see and appreciate who we really are. The obstacle to authentic expression is fear of judgment. However, like pheasants, we can learn to overcome this fear.

The call of the pheasants is also an effective means of communication. In our lives, the ability to communicate clearly is essential for building and maintaining healthy relationships. Expressing one's needs, desires, and concerns in an open and respectful manner improves mutual understanding and resolves conflicts.

MAKE YOURSELF HEARD Taking inspiration from the pheasant, use this exercise to express your authentic voice and practice until it becomes second nature.

1. Find a quiet, comfortable place to sit that is free from distractions. Close your eyes and gently take a few deep breaths to relax.
2. Think of an area in your life where you feel you are not fully expressing yourself. It could be at work, in relationships, or in any other situation.
3. Imagine that your voice is like the call of the pheasant. Visualize yourself speaking with confidence, expressing your thoughts and feelings with authenticity. Feel the energy and release that comes from using your voice.
4. Open your eyes, and using a notebook or tablet, write a short personal statement representing your authentic voice.
5. Every day, spend a few minutes practicing the expression of your authentic voice. This can include writing exercises, meditation, or simply talking to someone you trust.

THE COLDEST TIME

大寒

Daikan

PIERCING COLD.
ICE SCULPTS THE WORLD.
NATURE ON PAUSE.

JANUARY 20-24

THE BUTTERBUR SENDS UP SHOOTS

款冬華 *Fuki no hana saku*

Maintaining hope in times of difficulty guides us toward new opportunities for growth.

The *Fuki no hana saku* microseason marks the time when the butterbur, a perennial herbaceous plant, begins to sprout. The butterbur (*Petasites japonicus*) is one of the first signs of life to emerge from the cold winter soil, being a symbol of renewal and hope. This plant, which grows in moist, shady areas, is valued in Japan not only for its resilience but also for its medicinal and culinary uses. The growth of butterbur in harsh conditions reminds us that we can find ways to nourish our minds and spirits even in the most adverse circumstances. Just as this plant finds the nourishment it needs to grow in the cold, hard soil of winter, we too can find interior and external resources to sustain us. These can include:

Nourishing mind and spirit: Butterbur teaches us that even in the most adverse situations we can find ways to nourish and strengthen our minds and our spirit. This process of growth and adaptation repurposes resources, which we can cultivate through various practices.

Mindfulness: One of the most powerful resources for nurturing our minds is the practice of mindfulness. Being present in the moment and observing our thoughts without judgment helps us develop greater awareness of ourselves and our reactions. This awareness allows us to face difficulties with a more open and resilient mind, just like the butterbur that finds the strength to produce shoots in the frozen ground.

Connecting with loved ones: Relationships are another source of nourishment for our spirits. Emotional support and connection with friends and family members furnishes us with a sense of belonging, which is essential to our well-being. Maintaining and nurturing these relationships, through small gestures of affection and understanding, can make a big difference.

Learning new skills: The process of continuous learning helps us feel more competent and confident. Acquiring new skills or deepening existing ones enables us to face challenges with greater confidence. Like the butterfly who finds ways to grow in adverse conditions, we too can expand our capabilities and resources through learning.

Adopting a positive attitude: Maintaining a positive attitude is decisive for our mental well-being. This does not mean ignoring difficulties, but rather recognizing and accepting challenges as opportunities for growth. The butterbur, with its ability to flourish despite difficult conditions, teaches us that an attitude of hope and resilience can take us a long way.

A GUIDE TO NOURISHING THE MIND AND SPIRIT This mini guide offers practical tips and activities for cultivating an inner equilibrium by nurturing our mind and spirit. This takes commitment and awareness, but the benefits are invaluable. Experiment with the following practices and find out which ones work best for you. Remember that the key is continuity and commitment to taking care of yourself.

MINDFULNESS PRACTICES

- **Daily meditation:** Devote at least 10 minutes a day to meditation. Find a quiet place, sit comfortably, and focus on your breath.
- **Mindful breathing:** Find short breaks throughout the day to take a few deep breaths. Inhale slowly through your nose, hold for a few seconds, and exhale through your mouth. This helps calm the mind and reduce stress.

CONNECTING WITH NATURE

- **Walks in nature:** Spend time outdoors, even if it is just a short walk in the park. Nature has a calming and restorative effect on the mind.
- **Gardening:** Take care of a plant or nurture a container or small garden. Contact with the earth and seeing something grow under your care can be very rewarding and therapeutic.

RELATIONSHIP CARE

- **Quality time:** Spend quality time with loved ones. Actively listen, share your feelings, and create positive memories together.
- **Social support:** Don't hesitate to ask for support when you need it. Talk to friends, family members, or a professional if you feel the need to express preoccupations or difficulties.

CREATIVE ACTIVITIES

- **Reflective writing:** Keep a journal in which you note down thoughts, emotions, and reflections. Writing can help you process experiences and clarify your feelings.
- **Artistic activities:** Spend time on activities such as painting or music. Artistic expression frees the mind and nourishes the spirit.

BODY CARE

- **Exercise:** Take regular physical activity. Exercise not only improves physical health but also releases endorphins that help to improve your mood.
- **Balanced nutrition:** Eat a balanced diet, choosing nutritious foods that support both body and mind. Cut down on ultra-processed and sugary foods.

LEARNING AND PERSONAL GROWTH

- **Reading and studying:** Spend time reading books that stimulate the mind and inspire the spirit. Choose topics that interest and motivate you.

JANUARY 25–29

THICK ICE COVERS THE STREAMS

水沢腹堅 *Sawamizu kōri tsumeru*

In quiet moments, gather your energy and prepare yourself to emerge stronger and more determined than before.

Ice forming on the rivers and streams at this time of year is a powerful symbol of consolidation and stability. When water, which usually flows freely and is in constant motion, stops and solidifies, it represents a time to pause and gather energy. This natural phenomenon offers us an important psychological lesson: the need to stop, gather our strength, and build an inner refuge.

In our busy lives, it is easy to feel overwhelmed by continuous demands and changes. Just as water finds stability by turning into ice, we too can find a sense of security and stability when we learn to stop and consolidate our inner resources. This process involves building an inner refuge, a metaphorical place where we can gather our energy, reflect on our experiences, and prepare for future challenges.

Building an inner refuge means creating a safe and secure space within ourselves where we can take shelter in times of trouble. This space can be cultivated through mindfulness practices and personal reflection. Taking time to reflect on our experiences, acknowledge our emotions, and accept our thoughts without judgment is critical to our personal growth. This inner refuge becomes a source of strength, allowing us to face challenges with greater confidence and peace of mind.

Just as ice conserves water at a time of pause, we too can use periods of stillness to gather our energy. This means taking care of ourselves, both physically and mentally, and finding activities that nourish and regenerate us. This can be devoting time to a hobby we love, spending quality time with loved ones, or simply relaxing and recharging ourselves. Gathering our energy is not only about physical rest but also about finding balance and inner peace.

Consolidating our energies and building an internal refuge prepares us to face future challenges. Just as the ice in streams hardens in preparation for winter, we too can use these moments of pause to reflect on our goals and plan our next steps. This process of preparation allows us to be more resilient, so we are ready to face any difficulties that may occur, with a calm and focused mind.

CONSOLIDATE YOUR ENERGY This meditation is designed to help you create an inner sanctuary, a safe place where you can gather your energy and find stability and inner peace.

1. Sit in a quiet, comfortable place, free from distractions, where you can relax and focus on yourself.
2. Close your eyes and start to breathe deeply. Slowly inhale through your nose, hold your breath for a few seconds, then slowly exhale through your mouth. Repeat this sequence three times, allowing your body and mind to relax completely.
3. Imagine yourself in a peaceful winter landscape, with streams flowing past snow-covered trees. Visualize the water beginning to slow down and solidify, forming a shiny, transparent layer of ice. Feel yourself become part of this natural process of consolidation and calm.
4. Now, imagine building a safe haven within yourself. This place can be anything that makes you feel safe and tranquil: a cozy room, a cabin in the mountains, or a hidden corner in a garden. Fill it with objects and symbols that for you represent safety, peace, and strength.
5. Visualize yourself sitting in this refuge, surrounded by a sense of calm and protection. Imagine that you are gathering all your dispersed energies and consolidating them in your center, just as water transforms into ice. Feel how these energies strengthen you, creating stability and security inside you.

6. Take a few minutes to reflect on recent experiences, as well as your goals and desires. Use this quiet time to examine what is really important to you. Allow your mind to explore freely, acknowledging thoughts and emotions without judgment.
7. Imagine leaving your inner refuge, taking with you the calm and strength you have found. Visualize yourself facing future challenges with renewed determination and confidence. Feel how this preparation makes you more resilient and prepared for whatever comes.
8. When you feel ready, begin to slowly bring your attention back to the present. Take a few deep breaths and gradually open your eyes. Take a moment to appreciate the feeling of calm and security you have created within yourself.
9. Practice this meditation regularly to maintain a sense of calm and inner strength, just like the ice that forms on the streams, consolidating its energy for the winter.

JANUARY 30–FEBRUARY 3

THE HENS BEGIN TO LAY EGGS

鶏始乳 *Niwatori hajimete toya ni tsuku*

Nurturing our dreams with patience and care is the key to seeing them grow and flourish.

The microseason *Niwatori hajimete toya ni tsuku* marks the beginning of egg laying by hens, a symbol of renewal. This period invites us to reflect on the value of the care and dedication we devote to our ideas, projects, and relationships. Just as the hens take care of their eggs, we too must learn to nurture what we consider important. This season encourages us to dedicate time and energy to ensure our passions and connections grow and flourish, developing them through constant care.

This means not only having a clear and defined vision, but also constantly working to achieve it. Like a hen caring for her eggs, we must protect our ideas from negative influences and nurture them with information, skills, and resources that will help them grow.

Eggs take time to hatch and reveal the life within them. This natural process teaches us the importance of patience and the ability to wait confidently for our efforts to bear fruit. Not everything happens immediately; some things take time and care to develop. Learning to be patient allows us to appreciate the journey and understand that the value often lies in the waiting and the constant work we devote to our goals. Patience teaches us not to become discouraged by delays, but to see each moment as part of a larger process of growth and achievement.

In the natural world, cycles of growth and renewal follow a well-defined rhythm that cannot be accelerated without compromising balance. Hens' eggs, for example, must be incubated for a specific period before they can hatch. During this time, a stable environment and constant care are essential to ensure that the eggs develop properly. This principle can also be applied to our lives: we must recognize and respect the time required for our plans and ambitions to mature. Patience is a quality that enables us to navigate serenely through periods of waiting. It is the ability to remain calm and confident during this process, even when results are not immediately visible. Cultivating patience means learning to deal with frustration, accepting that each stage of life has its time, and that precious things require care and dedication. Waiting is not just a passive pause, but a period of preparation and inner growth. It allows us to reflect on our progress, review our goals, and strengthen our resolve. Waiting gives us the opportunity to hone our skills, accumulate knowledge, and build a solid foundation for future success. Accepting waiting as part of the journey helps us to live with greater awareness and appreciate every moment.

To cultivate patience, having faith in the process is essential. This means believing that our efforts and dedication will bring positive results. Remembering that every small action contributes to our ultimate goal gives us the strength to continue and not give up.

OUR INNER NEST This exercise is designed to help you cultivate patience and care for your projects and relationships. This exercise reminds us that, with dedication and patience, we can see our efforts flourish and achieve our goals, appreciating the journey and understanding that each moment is part of a larger process of growth and fulfillment.

1. Sit in a comfortable place, free from distractions, where you can unwind and focus.
2. Close your eyes and take a few deep breaths, inhaling slowly through your nose and exhaling through your mouth. Allow your body and mind to relax.
3. Imagine a cozy nest containing a few eggs. Each egg represents a project, idea, or relationship you care about.
4. Think about the projects or relationships you want to devote more attention and care to. Visualize yourself caring for the nest, protecting and nurturing the eggs with patience and dedication.
5. Open your eyes and in a notebook or tablet write down the feelings and thoughts that came to you during the exercise. Identify the areas of your life that require patience and care and note down an action plan to nurture them.
6. Choose one small action you can take today to begin caring for an important project or relationship. Commit to taking this step by the end of the day.
7. Every day, devote a few minutes to this visualization and reflection exercise. Take note of the progress you are making and the feelings you are experiencing. This will help you maintain a sense of continuity and steady growth.

CONCLUSION

Our journey through the 72 microseasons of the traditional Japanese calendar has provided a unique opportunity to connect with natural rhythms and reflect deeply on our personal and spiritual growth. Each microseason, with its specific teachings and psychological reflections, invited us to consider aspects of daily life through a more attentive and conscious lens.

We explored how the seasons and natural changes can act as a mirror for our internal experiences, illuminating lessons of resilience, adaptability, patience, and hope. These themes, intrinsically linked to the cycles of nature, remind us that every stage of life, however difficult, carries with it the potential for growth and renewal.

The principles of Zen psychology have guided us through the process of acceptance and personal growth, enabling us to navigate life's challenges with greater balance and serenity, and have provided us with practical tools to improve our psychological flexibility, enabling us to live more authentically and meaningfully. I hope this book has provided you with valuable insights to enrich your daily practice, inspired you to see beauty in the little things, and to find strength and resilience in times of difficulty. May you continue to cultivate your personal growth, just as nature cultivates its seasons, with patience, dedication, and a deep connection to the present.

Thank you for sharing this journey with me. May you find serenity, balance, and continued inspiration in the rhythm of the microseasons, reflecting the beauty and wisdom of nature in your life.

With gratitude,
Antonio, the Zen psychologist

INDEX

INDEX

ACKNOWLEDGEMENTS

Shutterstock.com/Rawpixel.com, pages 2 and 82; /Egle Lipeikaite, page 26; /Tanya Syrytsyna, pages 5, 133, and 138; /Eisfrei, page 166; /Susii, pages 20 and 74; /Yoguru, page 124; /Suibokuga Arai, page 76; /Natalia Koltsova, page 150; /Valumyan , pages 86 and 88; /Lauritta, pages 174 and 176; / marukopum, pages 99, 136 and 137.

Pages 16, 22, 28, 34, 40, 46, 52, 58, 64, 72, 80, 90, 98, 106, 112, 118, 126, 132, 140, 146, 152, 162, 172 and 180 from Rawpixel.com.